ENGLISH ✳ HERITAGE

Book of
Roman Forts
in Britain

ENGLISH ⊞ HERITAGE

Book of Roman Forts in Britain

Paul Bidwell

B. T. Batsford / English Heritage
London

© Paul Bidwell 1997

First published 1997

All rights reserved. No part of this publication
may be reproduced in any form or by any means,
without permission from the Publisher

Typeset by Bernard Cavender Design & Greenwood Graphics Publishing
Printed and bound in Great Britain by The Bath Press, Bath

Published by B.T. Batsford Ltd
583 Fulham Road, London SW6 5BY

A CIP catalogue record for this book is
available from the British Library

ISBN 0 7134 7099 2 (cased)
0 7134 7100 X (limp)

(Front cover) The Roman fort of Segedunum at Wallsend where
the eastern end of Hadrian's Wall runs into the river in the form
of a mole. The fort is shown in its third-century state with partly
blocked gates and a large hall added to the front of the
headquarters building. The *vicus* between the fort and river is
enclosed to the east by the final length of Hadrian's Wall (the
Branch Wall) and to the west by an earthen bank and ditches
located in recent excavations (it is possible but less likely that
these defences belonged to an annexe to the fort rather than to
the *vicus* defences). The existence of fields north of Hadrian's
Wall has also been proved by excavation.

(Back cover) Defensive pits *(lilia)*, probably once with sharpened
stakes set in their bases, which block the northern approach to
the fort of Rough Castle on the Antonine Wall.

Contents

Illustrations

Colour plates

Acknowledgements

In writing a general survey of this kind I owe a huge debt to those, past and present, who have studied and written about Roman forts in Britain and further afield. For more than a decade I have been fortunate enough to work with a team who share my interest in the Roman army in Britain, particularly Alex Croom, Bill Griffiths, Nick Hodgson and Margaret Snape: many of the topics in this book have been discussed with them, much to my benefit. Nick Hodgson for some years has shared responsibility with me for the excavations at South Shields; our discussions of the wider significance of the discoveries there have contributed much to the views set out in this book, which he has read and commented upon. I am also grateful for comments from Dr Stephen Johnson.

I am indebted to Roger Oram for preparing a number of illustrations (**1, 20, 21, 23, 26, 28–30, 33–5, 49, 60, 62, 64**). The following illustrations are reproduced with permission from: English Heritage (**22, 37, 40, 43, 46, 51, 53, 59, 68, 74, 77, colour plates 3, 8, 9, 12, cover illustration**); Tyne and Wear Museums (**15, 36, 39, 41, 48, 58, 63, 70, colour plate 4**); Exeter Archaeology (**16, colour plate 1**); Royal Commission on Historical Monuments, England (**17, 71**); Professor W. S. Hanson (**18**, drawing by Keith Speller); Colchester Archaeological Trust (**19**); Dr N. Hodgson (**25, 42, 55**); Carlisle Archaeological Unit (**27**); Dr Brenda Heywood (**47**); The Vindolanda Trust (**56**, photos by Alison Rutherford, copyright Vindolanda Trust); The Arbeia Society (Quinta) (**67, colour plate 11**); Cambridge University Collection of Air Photographs (**73**, copyright reserved); Museum of London Archaeological Service (**75**); Museum of Antiquities, University of Newcastle upon Tyne (**76**); J. Berry and D. J. A. Taylor (**79–80**); Groundwork South Tyneside (**colour plate 7**); and Mrs V. G. Swan (**colour plate 10**).

1
'Peace preserved by a constant preparation for war'

Roman forts as a part of Britain's archaeological heritage

The Roman Empire was created by the valour and discipline of the Roman army; in later times the incompetence, indiscipline and corruption of the army was in part responsible for extinguishing the western part of the Empire. That was the opinion of Edward Gibbon, justified at length in *The Decline and Fall of the Roman Empire* (published between 1776 and 1788), and of many others since. 'The terror of the Roman arms' allowed the Roman emperors to preserve 'peace by a constant preparation for war', according to Gibbon, and thus the study of the army has always occupied a central place in the history of the Roman Empire.

Between 40,000 and 50,000 soldiers, more than a tenth of the army's total strength, were stationed in Britain during the second century, out of all proportion to the size of the province; the governorship of Britain, which included the powers of army commander, was until the third century second in prestige only to that of Syria. Within fifty years of the conquest, military zones had been imposed across Britain, particularly in the thinly populated, upland areas – in Wales, northern England and southern Scotland. Many forts have not been built over since their abandonment by the Romans, nor have their remains been completely levelled in the search for re-usable building materials. Britain thus has many of the best-preserved forts to have survived from the Roman Empire.

In this book 298 military sites are listed, including fortresses (**1**); some in this list have successive forts on adjacent sites. There are more forts to be found: two new forts came to light in 1996 and many probably remain to be discovered, particularly in the Midlands, the Welsh borders and in south-west England. This large number of forts is explained by the half-century of intermittent campaigning starting in AD 43, which was required to establish control of Britain as far north as Scotland. Much of Scotland was abandoned in AD 86–7, but the temporary reoccupation of southern Scotland in the mid-second century added dozens more forts to the total.

The study of Roman forts in Britain has a long history. Many antiquaries, with their thorough grounding in the languages and literature of the Graeco-Roman world, were strongly drawn to the remains of Roman occupation in Britain. Once the study of the Roman provinces had been put on a proper footing, the importance of Britain's Roman military remains, in terms of both their number and state of preservation, became clear. Yet, despite more than a century of scientific excavations, the modern study of the Roman army in Britain is still much more than merely filling in the details of a picture complete in its essentials. From the middle of the eighteenth century, when General Roy was astonished to discover that the progress of the governor Agricola's campaigns in Scotland could actually be traced on the ground through the

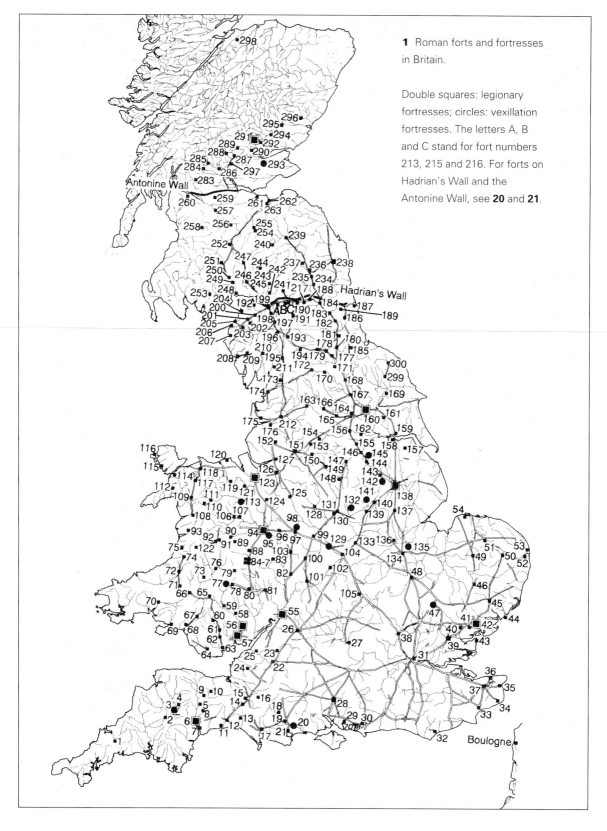

1 Roman forts and fortresses in Britain.

Double squares: legionary fortresses; circles: vexillation fortresses. The letters A, B and C stand for fort numbers 213, 215 and 216. For forts on Hadrian's Wall and the Antonine Wall, see **20** and **21**.

KEY

This list of forts and fortresses excludes supposed *burgi* (small late Roman forts on roads in the civilian areas), fortlets, watch towers and temporary works. It also excludes sites, particularly in southern Britain, where forts are thought likely but are not proven. Many sites include forts of different periods or fortresses replaced by forts, as at Usk. In several instances successive forts on nearby sites have been included under the same number, as at Roecliffe and Aldborough. Doubt attaches to some of these sites: for example, Cawdor is far to the north of any proven Roman fort but its existence is accepted on the basis of the interim reports so far published. Note that fort number 214 has subsequently been deleted (no longer considered a fort).

1 Nanstallon, Cornwall
2 Okehampton, Devon
3 North Tawton, Devon
4 Bury Barton, Devon
5 Tiverton, Devon
6 Exeter, Devon
7 Topsham, Devon
8 Cullompton, Devon
9 Clayhanger, Devon
10 Wiveliscombe, Somerset
11 Seaton, Devon
12 Axminster, Devon
13 Waddon Hill, Dorset
14 Ham Hill, Somerset
15 Ilchester, Somerset
16 South Cadbury, Somerset
17 Dorchester, Dorset
18 Hod Hill, Dorset
19 Shapwick, Dorset
20 Lake, Dorset
21 Hamworthy, Dorset
22 Bath, Avon
23 Nettleton Shrub, Wiltshire
24 Charterhouse, Somerset
25 Sea Mills, Avon
26 Cirencester, Gloucestershire
27 Dorchester-on-Thames, Oxfordshire
28 Silchester, Hampshire
29 Portchester, Hampshire
30 Fishbourne, West Sussex
31 Cripplegate, London
32 Pevensey, East Sussex
33 Lympne, Kent
34 Dover, Kent
35 Richborough, Kent
36 Reculver, Kent
37 Canterbury, Kent
38 Verulamium, Hertfordshire
39 Chelmsford, Essex
40 Kelvedon, Essex
41 Gosbecks, Essex
42 Colchester, Essex
43 Bradwell, Essex
44 Walton Castle, Suffolk
45 Baylam House, Suffolk
46 Ixworth, Suffolk
47 Great Chesterford, Essex
48 Godmanchester, Cambridgeshire
49 Saham Toney, Norfolk
50 Caistor St Edmund, Norfolk
51 Swanton Morley, Norfolk
52 Burgh Castle, Norfolk
53 Caister-on-Sea, Norfolk
54 Brancaster, Norfolk
55 Gloucester/Kingsholm, Gloucestershire
56 Usk, Gwent
57 Caerleon, Gwent
58 Abergavenny, Gwent
59 Pen-y-Gaer, Powys
60 Pen-y-Darren, Mid Glamorgan

61 Gelligaer, Mid Glamorgan
62 Caerphilly, Mid Glamorgan
63 Cardiff, South Glamorgan
64 Cowbridge, South Galmorgan
65 Y Gaer, Powys
66 Llandovery, Dyfed
67 Coelbren Gaer, West Glamorgan
68 Neath, West Glamorgan
69 Loughor, West Glamorgan
70 Carmarthen, Dyfed
71 Pumpsaint, Dyfed
72 Llanio, Dyfed
73 Caerau, Powys
74 Trawscoed, Dyfed
75 Pen Llwyn, Dyfed
76 Castell Collen, Powys
77 Clyro, Hereford and Worcester
78 Clifford, Powys
79 Walton, Powys
80 Kenchester, Hereford and Worcester
81 Stretton Grandison, Hereford and Worcester
82 Droitwich, Hereford and Worcester
83 Wall Town, Shropshire
84 Jay Lane, Hereford and Worcester
85 Leintwardine, Hereford and Worcester
86 Buckton, Hereford and Worcester
87 Brandon Camp, Hereford and Worcester
88 Stretford Bridge, Shropshire
89 Brompton, Shropshire
90 Forden Gaer, Powys
91 Llwyn-y-Brain, Powys
92 Caersws, Powys
93 Pennal, Gwynedd
94 Wroxeter, Shropshire
95 Leighton, Shropshire
96 Red Hill, Shropshire
97 Water Eaton, Staffordshire
98 Kinvaston, Staffordshire
99 Wall, Staffordshire
100 Metchley, Warwickshire
101 Alcester, Warwickshire
102 Baginton, Warwickshire
103 Greensforge, Staffordshire
104 Wigston Parva, Leicestershire
105 Towcester, Northamptonshire
106 Llansantffraid-ym-Mechain, Powys
107 Abertanat, Powys
108 Brithidir, Gwynedd
109 Tomen-y-Mur, Gwynedd
110 Caer Gai, Gwynedd
111 Llanfor, Gwynedd
112 Pen Llystyn, Gwynedd
113 Rhyn Park, Shropshire
114 Caernarvon, Gwynedd
115 Aberffraw, Anglesey
116 Caer Gybi, Anglesey
117 Caer Llugwy, Gwynedd
118 Caerhun, Gwynedd
119 Ruthin, Gwynedd
120 Prestatyn, Clwyd
121 Ffrith, Clwyd
122 Cae Gaer, Powys
123 Chester, Cheshire
124 Whitchurch, Shropshire
125 Chesterton, Staffordshire
126 Northwich, Cheshire
127 Wilderspool, Cheshire
128 Rocester, Staffordshire
129 Mancetter, Warwickshire
130 Strutts Park, Derbyshire
131 Derby, Derbyshire
132 Broxtowe, Nottinghamshire
133 Leicester, Leicestershire
134 Water Newton, Cambridgeshire
135 Longthorpe, Cambridgeshire
136 Great Casterton, Leicestershire
137 Ancaster, Lincolnshire
138 Lincoln, Lincolnshire
139 Margidunum, Nottinghamshire

140 Thorpe, Nottinghamshire
141 Osmanthorpe, Nottinghamshire
142 Newton-on-Trent, Lincolnshire
143 Marton, Lincolnshire
144 Bawtry, Nottinghamshire
145 Rossington, South Yorkshire
146 Doncaster, South Yorkshire
147 Templeborough, South Yorkshire
148 Chesterfield, Derbyshire
149 Brough-on-Noe, Derbyshire
150 Melandra Castle, Derbyshire
151 Manchester, Greater Manchester
152 Wigan, Greater Manchester
153 Castleshaw, Greater Manchester
154 Slack, West Yorkshire
155 Burghwallis, South Yorkshire
156 Castleford, West Yorkshire
157 Kirmington, Humberside
158 Winteringham, Humberside
159 Brough-on-Humber
160 York, North Yorkshire
161 Hayton, North Humberside
162 Roall, North Yorkshire
163 Elslack, North Yorkshire
164 Newton Kyme, North Yorkshire
165 Adel, West Yorkshire
166 Ilkley, West Yorkshire
167 Roecliffe/Aldborough, North Yorkshire
168 Healam Bridge, North Yorkshire
169 Malton, North Yorkshire
170 Wensley, North Yorkshire
171 Catterick, North Yorkshire
172 Brough-by-Bainbridge, North Yorkshire
173 Burrow-in-Lonsdale, Lancashire
174 Lancaster, Lancashire
175 Kirkham, Lancashire
176 Walton-le-Dale, Lancashire
177 Carkin Moor, North Yorkshire
178 Greta Bridge, North Yorkshire
179 Bowes, Durham
180 Piercebridge, Durham
181 Binchester, Durham
182 Lanchester, Durham
183 Ebchester, Durham
184 Corbridge, Northumberland
185 Elstob, Durham
186 Chester-le-Street, Durham
187 South Shields, Tyne and Wear
188 Newbrough, Northumberland
189 Whickham, Tyne and Wear
190 Haltwhistle Burn, Northumberland
191 Whitley Castle, Northumberland
192 Kirkbride, Cumbria
193 Kirkby Thore, Cumbria
194 Brough, Cumbria
195 Low Borrowbridge, Cumbria
196 Brougham, Cumbria
197 Old Penrith, Cumbria
198 Wreay, Cumbria
199 Carlisle, Cumbria
200 Old Carlisle, Cumbria
201 Blennerhasset, Cumbria
202 Caermote, Cumbria
203 Papcastle, Cumbria
204 Beckfoot, Cumbria
205 Maryport, Cumbria
206 Burrow Walls, Cumbria
207 Moresby, Cumbria
208 Ravenglass, Cumbria
209 Hardknott, Cumbria
210 Ambleside, Cumbria
211 Watercrook, Cumbria
212 Ribchester, Lancashire
213 Old Church, Brampton, Cumbria
214 [entry deleted] Castle Hill, Boothby
215 Nether Denton, Cumbria
216 Throp, Cumbria
217 Vindolanda, Northumberland
218 Wallsend, Tyne and Wear
219 Newcastle upon Tyne, Tyne and Wear
220 Benwell, Tyne and Wear

221 Rudchester, Northumberland
222 Haltonchesters, Northumberland
223 Chesters, Northumberland
224 Carrawburgh, Northumberland
225 Housesteads, Northumberland
226 Great Chesters, Northumberland
227 Carvoran, Northumberland
228 Birdoswald, Cumbria
229 Castlesteads, Cumbria
230 Stanwix, Cumbria
231 Burgh-by-Sands, Cumbria
232 Drumburgh, Cumbria
233 Bowness, Cumbria
234 Risingham, Northumberland
235 Blakehope, Northumberland
236 High Rochester, Northumberland
237 Chew Green, Northumberland
238 Learchild, Northumberland
239 Newstead, Borders
240 Oakwood, Borders
241 Bewcastle, Cumbria
242 Netherby, Cumbria
243 Broomholm, Dumfries and Galloway
244 Raeburnfoot, Dumfries and Galloway
245 Birrens, Dumfries and Galloway
246 Ladyward, Dumfries and Galloway
247 Milton, Dumfries and Galloway
248 Ward Law, Dumfries and Galloway
249 Carzield, Dumfries and Galloway
250 Dalswinton, Dumfries and Galloway
251 Drumlanrig, Dumfries and Galloway
252 Crawford, Strathclyde
253 Glenlochar, Dumfries and Galloway
254 Easter Happrew, Borders
255 Lyne, Borders
256 Castledykes, Strathclyde
257 Loudoun Hill, Strathclyde
258 Bothwellhaugh, Strathclyde
259 Mollins, Strathclyde
260 Barochan Hill, Strathclyde
261 Cramond, Lothian
262 Elginhaugh, Lothian
263 Inveresk, Lothian
264 Carriden, Central
265 Inveravon, Central
266 Mumrills, Central
267 Falkirk, Central
268 Rough Castle, Central
269 Castlecary, Strathclyde
270 Westerwood, Strathclyde
271 Croy Hill, Strathclyde
272 Bar Hill, Strathclyde
273 Auchendavy, Strathclyde
274 Kirkintilloch, Strathclyde
275 Cadder, Strathclyde
276 Balmuildy, Strathclyde
277 Bearsden, Strathclyde
278 Castlehill, Strathclyde
279 Duntocher, Strathclyde
280 Old Kilpatrick, Strathclyde
281 Bishopton, Strathclyde
282 Camelon, Central
283 Drumquhassle, Central
284 Lake of Menteith, Central
285 Bochastle, Tayside
286 Doune, Central
287 Strageath, Tayside
288 Dalginross, Tayside
289 Fendoch, Tayside
290 Bertha, Tayside
291 Inchtuthil, Tayside
292 Cargill, Tayside
293 Carpow, Tayside
294 Cardean, Tayside
295 Inverquharity, Tayside
296 Stracathro, Tayside
297 Ardoch, Tayside
298 Cawdor, Grampian

survival of temporary camps as earthworks, the study of the Roman army in Britain has been marked by leaps in knowledge beyond the imagination of previous generations of scholars. This has continued down to the present with the discovery of an archive of military documents from Vindolanda, something no one would have thought possible, let alone dared hope for.

The archaeologist of today is presented with a mass of evidence about the Roman army in Britain which allows its history to be explored on many different levels. Many approaches can be adopted, but they all lead to greater understanding of an institutionalized society that is unique in the history of Europe: a standing army that garrisoned forts from Scotland to the eastern shores of the Black Sea and which held together much of Europe, North Africa and the Near East under a unified system of government.

The purpose of this book is to show how the military, economic and social histories of Roman forts and their occupants can be recovered from the wreck of antiquity. The emphasis is on the auxiliary forts occupied from the second century onwards. They are essential to understanding how the Roman army established the long-term military control over frontier areas on which the security of the Empire depended. The much larger legionary fortresses are a separate study and are mentioned mainly to supplement information from auxiliary forts. The remains of the Roman army in the field – marching camps and siege works – also fall outside the scope of this book. One important topic relevant to everyday life in the fort but not dealt with here is the religion of the Roman army. For the most part it sprang from the provincial and imperial religious systems, but with important modifications to reinforce military loyalty. The subject is complex and cannot be dealt with adequately in the confines of this book.

Four centuries of study

In the later sixteenth century the history and remains of the Roman Empire began to assume considerable importance for scholars in Britain. Under the Tudor dynasty the relationships between the church, people and monarchy had been abruptly and sometimes bloodily transformed; the history of Scotland, still at that time an independent nation, was if anything still more turbulent. The Roman Empire, although it had perished a thousand years earlier in western Europe, came to be seen as a symbol of the stability which could be achieved by the imposition of a system of laws on very diverse peoples.

The sixteenth century also saw the emergence of the antiquary, the student of early history and its remains. John Leland (?–1552) was Henry VIII's designated antiquary and his *Itineraries* mention Roman remains. However, the greatest of the early antiquaries was William Camden (1551–1623) who in his *Britannia* (1586) attempted to recover the geography of Roman Britain, relying on his own observations made in journeys around the country and on information from correspondents. The result was a study which went through six editions in Camden's lifetime and continued in revised versions until the early nineteenth century.

A hundred years or more were to elapse before special studies were made of Roman military antiquities, but the problems Camden faced in trying to make sense of Roman remains were much the same as those which confronted his successors. Most of the major ancient sources which described the Roman army and campaigns in Britain were at the disposal of Camden, as were the Roman geographies and itineraries, with the exception of the *Ravenna Cosmography*, not published until 1688. However, the ancient writers, although they described Roman camps for armies on campaign, had very little to say about the permanent forts which the antiquaries encountered. As far as the history of Britain as a Roman province was concerned, there was a reasonable coverage of the period of conquest under Claudius and Nero and a detailed account of the years from AD 77/8 to 83/4 in Tacitus' fulsome study of the career of his father-in-law, Gnaeus Iulius Agricola, as governor of Britain, but the following three centuries attracted only intermittent attention from Roman authors. Hadrian's Wall, for example, was not mentioned until the fourth century, some 200 years after it was built.

The study of place-names, particularly those of forts, was perplexing even when the modern name was derived from that mentioned in an ancient source. Camden, through the knowledge which he acquired of Welsh, was able to suggest the meanings of some Romano-British names and to understand the ancient derivations of names such as Winchester. Place-names were to become an obsession for the antiquaries, but few were as well equipped as Camden to make sense of them.

In the field there was enormous scope for the misidentification of archaeological sites. Inigo Jones, architect to Charles I, believed Stonehenge to have been a Roman temple and the most competent antiquaries sometimes mistook prehistoric hillforts and medieval mottes for Roman fortifications. The tendency was always to attribute impressive ancient earthworks to the genius of the Romans. The same was true of finds such as fine metalwork; as late as the mid-nineteenth century, Bronze Age swords and spearheads were ascribed a Roman date, as in Stuart's *Caledonia Romana* of 1852 (although in fairness he admitted that they might be much earlier). Once the antiquaries put aside their books and took to the saddle, they travelled through a landscape mapped only in the barest outline by their contemporaries and filled with remains, many of which could not be explained. They explored the past without most of the chronological signposts we now take for granted. In the face of all these frustrations the impetus to continue their work of discovery and description came above all from a sense of awe at what had survived. There is no better expression of this than Camden's account of Hadrian's Wall: 'verily I have seene the tract of it over the high

pitches and steepe descent of hills, wonderfully rising and falling' (Holland's translation of 1610).

Camden's work had laid the foundations for the study of Roman military remains. In 1695 a new edition of *Britannia* by Bishop Gibson (1669–1748) appeared, encouraging an upsurge of enthusiasm for Roman antiquities. In 1732 the Rev. John Horsley's *Britannia Romana* was published; it consisted of a history of Roman Britain concentrating largely on military matters, which was followed by accounts of Hadrian's Wall and the Antonine Wall and their forts, catalogues of inscriptions and sculptures, and finally an essay on the geography of the province. The work of a meticulous and acute observer, who by his own account travelled several thousand miles on his 'expensive and tedious' quest, Britannia Romana is notable for its analytical approach (2). Horsley was not merely content to describe, and his study of Hadrian's Wall shows his qualities to their best advantage. His fieldwork established the general spacing of forts and milecastles and he used finds of inscriptions naming units to identify the forts named in the late Roman army list, the *Notitia Dignitatum*. His study of forts indicated that nearby 'there were usually other buildings forming a sort of town ... inhabited by Britons to which the station [fort] was in the nature of a citadel, where the soldiers lodged and kept garrison'. An excessive faith in the consistency of Roman military terms sometimes led him up a blind alley, as in his attempts to distinguish various sites as examples of *stationes*, *castra aestiva* and *hiberna*, and *castella*. The general ignorance of archaeological remains also led him into error when he identified the fine medieval motte at Elsdon in Northumberland as a Roman fort because of the discovery of a Roman inscription which in fact had no doubt been brought to the motte from the nearby fort of Risingham as building material.

A few years earlier Alexander Gordon (1692–1754) had published his *Itinerarium Septentrionale* (1726/7), which not only covered

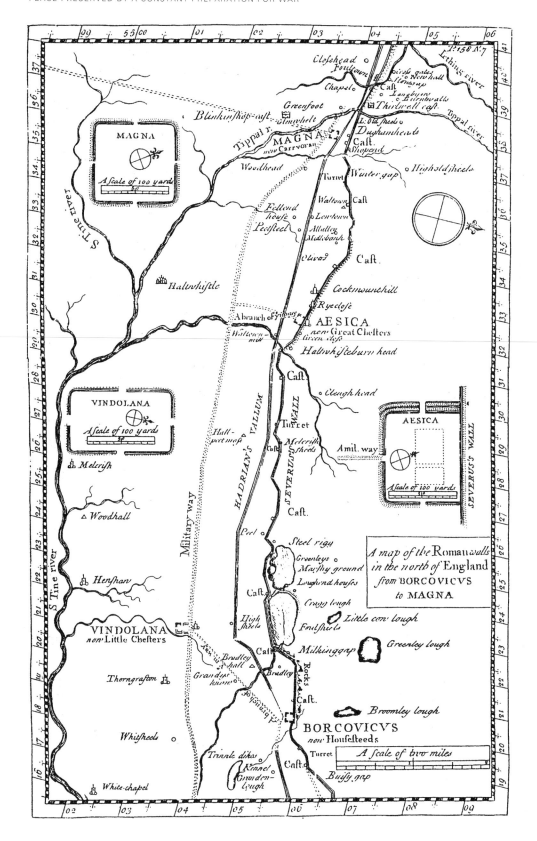

2 Hadrian's Wall from Housesteads to Carvoran, from Horsley's *Britannia Romana* (1732). The Roman names of the forts have been correctly identified, but Hadrian's Wall is attributed to Severus.

some of the same ground as *Britannia Romana*, but also, as a result of their acquaintance with each other, contained many of Horsley's ideas presented without acknowledgement and sometimes in a garbled form. Although this intellectual robbery has weighed heavily against Gordon, there is still much of value in his work. He was a good observer and published the first known plan of a temporary camp, that at Dalginross in Scotland (**3**); Horsley's plan of the site was botched and misnamed. He lacked Horsley's depth of scholarship but seems to

have been well acquainted with antiquities of many periods, noting that hillforts also occurred in Ireland and so could not be the work of the Roman army.

There were other remarkable figures at that time, notably William Stukeley, but, as far as the study of Roman military remains is concerned, Horsley towers above them all. He claimed in his Preface that the *Britannia Romana* 'contains the first history we have of Britain which can be rely'd on ... the original and foundation of the true history of our island'. His work was also the 'original and

3 Gordon's plan of the temporary camp at Dalginross, Perthshire, from his *Itinerarium Septentrionale* (1726/7); the enclosure to the left is a Flavian fort.

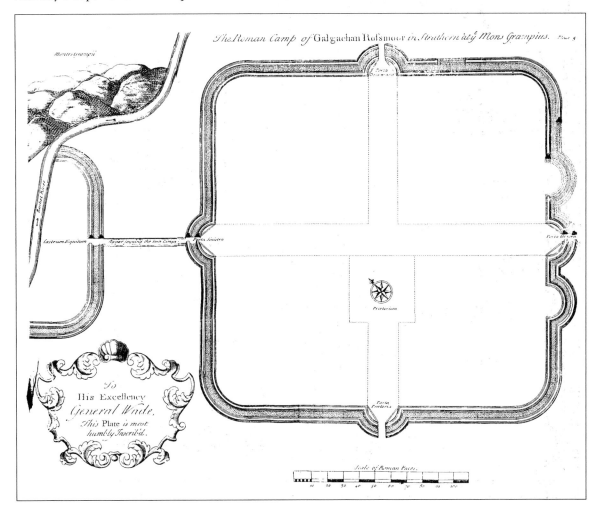

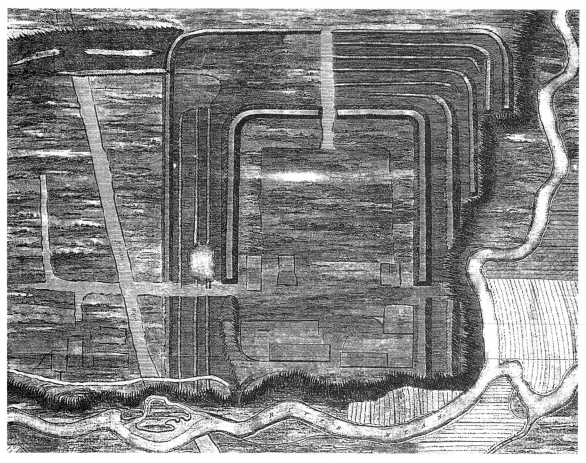

4 The fort at Birrens, a survey by General William Roy published in his *Military Antiquities* (1793). The Antonine fort is shown with a contemporary annexe to the west.

foundation' of Roman military archaeology in Britain and many of the problems which still command the attention of scholars were first recognized by Horsley.

Gordon and Horsley had shown how extensive were the remains of the Roman army in parts of northern Britain. Further discoveries were made in the aftermath of the 1745 rebellion, when the government decided that the highlands of Scotland 'should be thoroughly explored and laid open, by establishing military posts in [their] inmost recesses, and carrying roads of communication to [their] remotest parts'. Points of resemblance have been seen between the Hanoverian and Roman settlements of Scotland, and it is understandable that at that

time there was particular interest in Agricola's campaigns. Robert Melville made a careful study of Tacitus' *Agricola* and then searched for the route of Agricola's army 'combining what relates to the two later campaigns with the nature of the country and the Reason of War'. He consulted Gordon's *Itinerarium Septentrionale* and other works, and asked the military surveyors whether they had encountered any Roman camps beyond the Tay; but three years were to pass before a casual enquiry led him to four temporary camps in Strathmore. General William Roy (1726–90) had been planning known Roman forts such as Castledykes and Birrens (**4**) during the course of his work as a military surveyor on the new map of Scotland ordered by the government. He received the news of the discovery of temporary camps with delighted astonishment 'that, at the distance of so many ages, the remains of works so very temporary in their nature might be found to exist; much less could he [Roy] imagine, from a number of vestiges being discovered in succession to each other, at proper distances, that the daily marches of a Roman army might thereby be traced'.

Melville's discoveries greatly enlarged the scope of Roy's work. In his *Military Antiquities of the Romans in North Britain*, published posthumously in 1793, plans of a number of temporary camps were included, and attempts were made to understand the arrangement of their gates by reference to the descriptions by Polybius and Hyginus of the internal plans of camps for Roman armies on the march.

During the two centuries following the appearance of Camden's *Britannia* in 1586, progress had largely been concerned with topography: the surface remains of Roman forts were surveyed and described and the lines of Roman roads and frontier works established. Advances in knowledge came slowly and sprung from the obsession of a few individuals. For Camden Roman Britain was important because of the political difficulties of his times, and not least because attempts could be made to justify the existence of the Anglican Church by reference to a primitive Church in early Britain independent of the Bishop of Rome. Although religious controversy was not extinguished when Gordon and Horsley were writing, in an age when classical influences were strong, their chauvinism was confined to showing that Britain preserved Roman remains no less interesting than those of continental Europe (5). Roy, an officer who founded his career on military map-making, was a technocrat in an army dominated by aristocratic privilege, and it is natural that he should have been drawn to the remains of a more ancient army regarded as a model of efficiency and rational organization.

By the beginning of the nineteenth century the study of Roman military remains was well established, indeed so much so that it was subjected to gentle mockery. In *The Antiquary* (1816) Walter Scott made gentle fun of Jonathan Oldbuck, the antiquary of the title and embodiment of Scott's own antiquarian interests, who, guided by the writings of Gordon, sought out the site of Mons Graupius, the great battle between Agricola's army and the Caledonians. As the century progressed, detailed studies of individual forts or groups of forts began to appear. The Rev. John Hodgson (1779–1845) took up the study of the Wall where Horsley had left off and in perhaps the longest footnote in the history of publishing (168 pages) produced a new account in which the Wall, Vallum and forts were all for the first time correctly ascribed to Hadrian. In collaboration with Anthony Hedley (1777–1835) and others, he was also the first antiquary of established reputation to excavate Roman forts and to publish thoughtful accounts of the results. At Housesteads he excavated the temple of Mithras and some of the gates and interior buildings; at Vindolanda he worked with Anthony Hedley on the excavation of the gates and walls and on the baths of the

5 Views of the north gate (left), with wheel ruts in the threshold (b), and part of a bath house at Maryport, published in *Archaeologia* (1792). This is one of the earliest detailed representations of fort structures.

Circular tower at the angle of the W. and S.W. wall

6 Circular projecting tower at the south-west corner of the fort at Richborough, from Roach Smith's *The Antiquities of Richborough, Reculver and Lympne in Kent* (1850).

commanding officer's house. The latter described these excavations as an attempt to 'throw a very interesting and desirable light on the stationary economy of the Romans, and on the form and arrangement of their *castra stativa*'. In the 1850s Charles Roach Smith (1807–90) published accounts of the forts of the Saxon Shore at Richborough, Reculver, Lympne and Pevensey (6). His work is notable not only for careful descriptions of the structural remains but also for the attention that he paid to finds such as coins, pottery, glass and metal objects. In 1862 excavations and finds at the legionary fortress of Caerleon in Wales were published by John Edward Lee (1808–87).

Much of this work was purely descriptive, although, when the evidence allowed, historical conclusions were attempted, as in Hodgson's attribution of the Roman Wall to Hadrian. But for more than a century following the publication of Horsley's *Britannia Romana*, very little was known about the interior arrangements of Roman forts and Hedley's 'stationary economy of the Romans'. Then in 1852 and 1855 the outpost fort of High Rochester was excavated under the patronage of the fourth Duke of Northumberland. For the first time anywhere in the Roman Empire the greater part of a fort plan was recovered (7). Sadly, the excavators lacked any means of distinguishing the various periods of construction and the resulting plan made little sense. This seems to have dampened expectations and it was to be twenty years before work on this scale was carried out again. In 1857 Henry Maclauchlan produced a new survey of Hadrian's Wall commissioned by the Duke of Northumberland and smaller scale excavations continued.

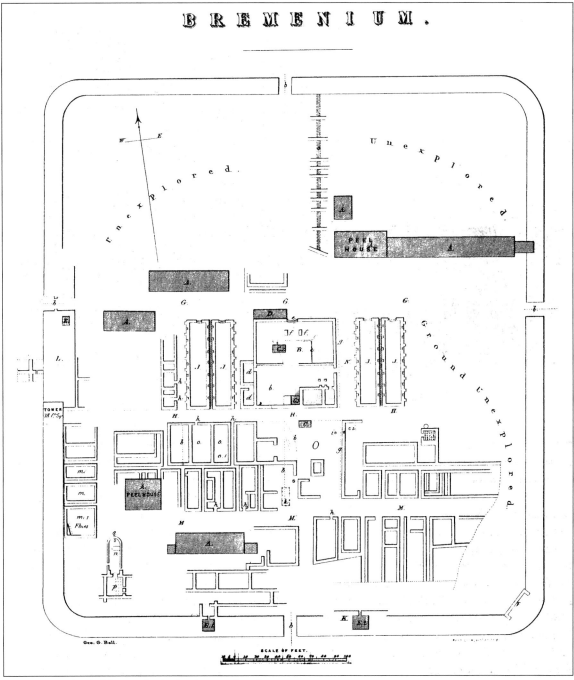

7 Plan of the fort at High Rochester following excavations in 1852 and 1855.

In 1875 the fields in which the fort at South Shields lay began to be developed for housing and what was perhaps the earliest large-scale rescue excavation on a site of any period in Britain was carried out (8). Once again little sense was made of the discoveries, this time because most of the buildings explored were the granaries of the great third-century supply-base, the function of which was not understood for many years to come, but the work was published by Robert Hooppell (1833–97) in some detail.

8 The forecourt of the late third- or early fourth-century headquarters building at South Shields, as excavated in April to May 1875; to the left, rubble from the collapsed front wall of the cross hall; to centre right, table altar in a rectangular recess, possibly part of a late Roman church.

Real progress in understanding Roman forts depended on two developments. The first was the informed analysis of building plans, leading to the identification of buildings' functions; this approach was developed successfully in Germany where architects and military engineers were involved in the state-sponsored investigations of the Roman frontier. The second development, essential to recovering the history of forts with several periods of construction, was an understanding of archaeological stratigraphy. The two decades before the outbreak of the First World War saw the rudiments of the necessary techniques being developed in Scotland and the north of England. Some in fact had already been developed by General Pitt Rivers in his excavations on Cranborne Chase and elsewhere in Wessex, but the northern archaeologists seem to have been largely ignorant of them. The first steps were taken in Scotland. In 1895 the fort of Birrens was excavated and buildings laid out to an orderly plan were exposed. The excavators realized that they were barracks, although of an unusual design which is still not fully understood. Nevertheless, confronted with an example of rational planning, the excavators then proceeded to deduce the units of measurement by which the buildings had been laid out. Equally important were the excavations at Ardoch in 1896–7 where the remains of buildings with timber frameworks were recognized for the first time. At an early stage in the work, 'low, narrow tracks in the till, apparently the beds once occupied by some kind of foundation' were seen. A few weeks later the clerk of works noticed a series of voids in the 'tracks' which proved to be the impressions of vertical posts set in foundation trenches, the remains of timber buildings typical of forts and fortresses in the first century and of the forts of the Antonine Wall.

Extensive excavations also took place on Hadrian's Wall at Great Chesters and Housesteads. The work was not technically accomplished but at Housesteads R. C. Bosanquet recovered the interior plan of the fort in outline (9); for many decades this was widely cited as the typical fort plan. By the time of the Housesteads excavations it was possible to take advantage of work on the Roman frontier in Germany and to compare the barracks and granary at Housesteads with those uncovered at the legionary fortress at Neuss. Of equal importance was German scholarship: Theodor

Mommsen had demonstrated that detailed study of the provinces was essential to an understanding of the history of Rome. His approach was eagerly adopted by Francis Haverfield (1860–1919) who in 1892 obtained an academic post at Oxford and thus became the first professional specialist in Romano-British archaeology. He carried out few excavations, but he played an important part in the exploration of the western part of Hadrian's Wall, work which was notable for its careful planning and detailed observation, including publication of sections printed in colour. His main interest was the study of inscriptions, but

9 Plan of Housesteads. As a result of the excavations in 1898, the first complete comprehensible plan of a fort was recovered. The Housesteads plan is not typical: forts of this period were usually less elongated and barracks are more commonly found aligned across the width of a fort (cf **14**); the fort was probably built for 800 men with no cavalry (a *cohors milliaria peditata*), one of the less common sizes of unit.

in his work on samian ware he began to provide archaeologists with what soon became the most important method of dating sites in the first and second centuries. Others took up this study and soon it became possible to distinguish, for example, Agricolan forts from those dating to the reigns of Trajan or Hadrian according to the styles of decoration on samian ware. At the same time the study of coarse pottery was put on a systematic basis.

The early years of the twentieth century saw an increase in the number of excavations: the most significant were at Newstead, Corbridge,

Haltwhistle Burn, Ambleside and Melandra Castle (**10**), and in Wales at Gelligaer. Most were published in considerable detail; they show a growing awareness of the importance of recording the contexts of finds and occasional attempts to record stratigraphy. The inter-war period saw great advances. Between 1921 and 1927 Mortimer Wheeler excavated the forts of Brecon Gaer and Caernarvon and the amphitheatre at the legionary fortress at Caerleon. At this stage in his career his techniques differed little from those of pre-war archaeologists in spite of his later strictures on their work. The sites were stripped and little attention was paid to archaeological stratification; for example only four sections were published from Caernarvon, and only one,

10 An early attempt at archaeological reconstruction; conjectural view of the fort at Melandra Castle and (inset) a gate and part of the headquarters forecourt.

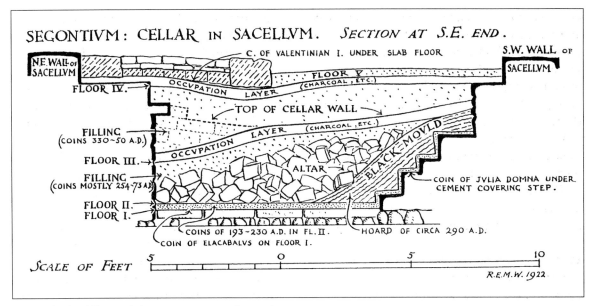

through the filling of the strongroom, showed any useful detail (**11**). The full development of his technique, as seen in his classic excavation of the Iron Age hill fort of Maiden Castle in Dorset, lay in the future.

The main focus of attention was on Hadrian's Wall where F. G. Simpson, Eric Birley, Ian Richmond and others, in a brilliant campaign of fieldwork, recovered a history of the Wall and its forts which was unchallenged until the late 1960s. Birley and Richmond complemented each other in their abilities and areas of interest. Birley was perhaps the foremost scholar of the Roman army in his era and in the 1930s was developing its prosopographical study, using the careers of individual officers to elucidate the structure of the army. He combined this with research into the history of forts, relying on penetrating study of old sources and the study of pottery, particularly samian ware; in these areas his approach was that of Haverfield. Richmond's strengths lay in his knowledge of the physical remains of the Roman army throughout the Empire which he combined with formidable, if sometimes idiosyncratic, abilities in the field, particularly as an excavator (**12**).

Sometimes in collaboration but often separately, Birley and Richmond dealt with

11 Vertical section through the filling of the strongroom of the headquarters building at Caernarvon, 1923. Wheeler concluded from his analysis of the stratigraphy that the building had been abandoned in the late third century and refurbished at the beginning of the fourth century.

12 Sir Ian Richmond, 1902–65, an excavator with unparalleled knowledge of Roman military remains.

13 A pause during the excavation of a late Roman barrack at Birdoswald in 1929. An 'altar' has been erected and Kurt Stade, a German archaeologist, third from right, is offering a sacrifice; left from Stade is Ian Richmond, and left from him is R. G. Collingwood, with Eric Birley in hat and with pipe, pointing to the altar. The next day the upper surface of the slab on which the 'altar' stood was seen to carry an early third-century inscription recording the construction of a granary. When the slab to the right, with two people standing on it, was raised, it too proved to be an inscription, recording the restoration of the commanding officer's house, headquarters buildings and baths at a date between AD 297 and 305. These inscriptions were used to determine the dates of two major building periods on Hadrian's Wall.

most of what seemed to be the main problems concerning Hadrian's Wall. Their first main joint venture at Birdoswald was crowned with the success that had eluded previous excavators: the recovery of two building inscriptions which supplied the dates of two intermediate periods in the history of the Wall (**13**). One inscription described the building of a granary in *c.* AD 205–7 and the other a restoration of the commanding officer's house together with baths and the headquarters building at a date between AD 296 and 305. At the time it was assumed that such new buildings or restorations would have followed destruction wrought by barbarian invasions. Therefore, when a fort or milecastle on Hadrian's Wall was excavated, three layers of destruction preceding rebuilding would be found (the third destruction, known from ancient sources, occurred in the Picts' War of AD 367).

By the late 1930s the chronologies of many Roman sites in Wales, northern England and Scotland were known in some detail. The largest gap in knowledge concerned southern England, where few sites associated with the early stages of the Roman conquest were known. This was remedied in the decades following the Second World War (see Chapter 8).

2
The plans and functions of forts

Fort plans

Any account of Roman forts must begin with an explanation of their plans. The example chosen for the purpose of illustration is Wallsend (*Segedunum*) which lies at the eastern end of Hadrian's Wall; it was built in the middle of the AD 120s, apparently for a *cohors quingenaria equitata* (a unit of 480 men with an additional 120 cavalry), which is the most common type of auxiliary unit (**14**). There is no such thing as a fort plan which is typical in every detail, but Wallsend, which was part of a vast programme of military engineering that included fifteen forts on the line of the Wall as well as a number to the south, is the most extensively excavated Hadrianic fort; its plan was largely replicated at South Shields some forty years later.

The characteristic features of the plan are its playing-card shape (with at Wallsend an area of 1.7ha or 4.1 acres) and the presence of a gate in each side. The smaller, fifth gate on the west side is a unique feature of forts which straddle Hadrian's Wall, providing additional access at the rear of the Wall. At such forts there are normally two smaller gates opposite each other, but at Wallsend the Wall changes direction to run down to the River Tyne which meant that a smaller east gate was omitted. The defences consist of a stone wall probably 4–4.5m (13–15ft) in height backed by an earth bank and with one or more defensive ditches beyond it. At the corners of the fort and at intervals along the fort wall there are towers. The typical T-shaped

plan of the interior is formed by the street (*via principalis*) running between the gates (*portae principales*) in the long side of the fort and that (*via praetoria*) running from the front gate of the fort (*porta praetoria*). At the junction of these streets stands the headquarters building (*principia*). Behind the headquarters building a street (*via decumana*) runs to the rear gate (*porta decumana*). Except in some rare circumstances these features occur in all forts built in Britain until the early third century, whether they are fortresses of some 20ha (50 acres) with accommodation for some 5,500 legionaries or forts less than a tenth of that size built to house 480 lower-grade auxiliaries. At Wallsend the headquarters building is flanked on its right by the commander's house and on its left by granaries, a standard arrangement (following Roman practice, left and right are cited from the position of an observer looking towards the front of the fort). A less common feature is the wide space behind these buildings. The odd position of the hospital, the courtyard building at the left-hand end of the central range, might have resulted from an alteration to the original scheme. The areas in front of and behind the headquarters building are filled with barracks, stables and workshops. There seem to have been eight barracks, five in the front part of the fort and three to the rear; these accommodated six centuries of foot soldiers,

14 Plan of the Hadrianic fort at Wallsend.

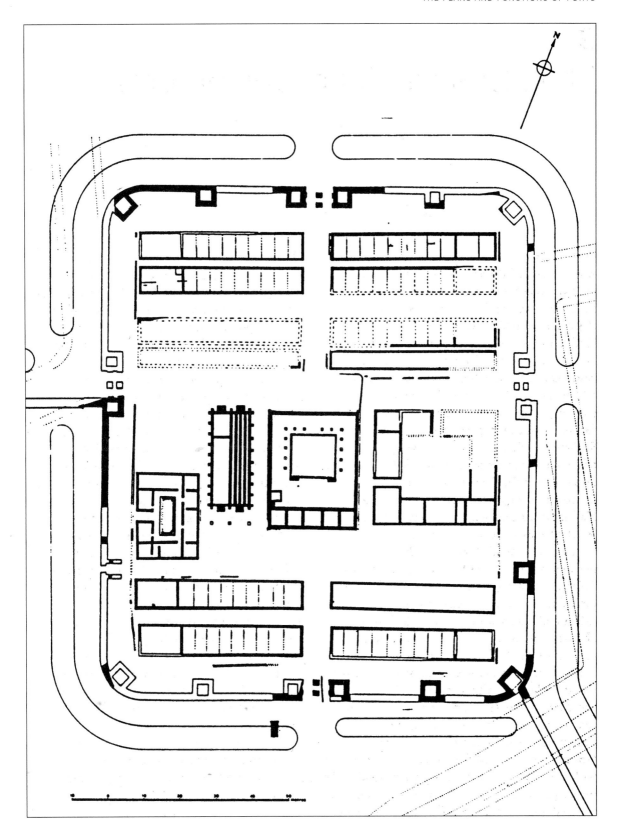

each with a strength of eighty men, and four groups of cavalry, each with thirty men, two groups to a barrack. The two remaining large buildings are probably stables; the building in the front part of the fort remains largely unexcavated but that in the rear part was found to be without partitions and contained a series of drains. The two narrow buildings facing the buildings of the central range are workshops.

Wallsend represents an advanced stage in the development of the fort. By the middle of the second century BC the Roman army was building fortified camps with regularly planned buildings to serve as winter quarters or siege bases, such as those which have been excavated at Numantia in Spain. The processes by which these early camps of the Roman Republic developed into the forts and fortresses built in such large numbers throughout the Roman Empire are obscure but the transformation had been completed before the conquest of Britain in AD 43. Although there were significant developments in the plans of buildings and defences, the essentials of fort plans in Britain did not change until the late Roman period.

Building a fort

In the first and second centuries AD the legions built fortifications of all types. They were responsible not only for the construction of Hadrian's Wall, the Antonine Wall and their own fortresses, but also for the construction of auxiliary forts, as many building stones and tiles with legionary name-stamps testify. The earliest evidence for auxiliaries engaged in building activities occurs in a Vindolanda writing-tablet from a level dated c. AD 95–105 which lists eighteen builders sent to the baths and mentions plasterers and activities connected with kilns, clay, lead and rubble. A letter of the same general period concerns the movement by wagon of large quantities of stone. In the third century AD, to which most building inscriptions from forts belong, auxiliaries were usually responsible for repairs and new buildings in their own forts (**15**).

Most military building projects required a heavy input of labour but little technical skill. The standards of construction encountered in forts are often very poor. Buildings are frequently put up on sites which have not been properly prepared, with the result that walls sink into the soft fills of earlier pits and ditches; foundations are skimped or omitted altogether; sub-standard building materials are employed and, even in the case of important structures such as gates, the exposed stonework is left half-finished. Examples of technical accomplishment, such as the road bridge at Chesters, the store house on site XI at Corbridge and the great buildings of legionary fortresses, shine out against the prevailing background of botched work.

Building materials usually came from the immediate locality. It has been cautiously estimated that a timber fort would have required the felling of 6.5–12.5ha (16–30 acres) of productive woodland to supply the necessary structural timbers. The change from timber to stone construction in Wales and northern Britain in the Trajanic and Hadrianic periods probably had much to do with the availability of good building stone. In areas where suitable quarries were only to be found at some distance, as in the case of some forts on the western part of Hadrian's Wall, construction in stone was delayed until the later second century.

A fort's plan was laid out by military surveyors. Two axes intersecting at right angles were established first, fixing the position of the *via principalis* and *viae praetoria* and *decumana*; then the line of the defences was laid out, and also the position of the minor streets within the fort which delimited the building plots. The use of standard units of measurement in the plans of forts was deduced long ago, as at Gellygaer in 1903, but the subject of mensuration has recently received much further study. It offers the prospect of reconstructing in outline entire plans where only fragments have been recovered by excavation, and is of particular importance in

15 Inscription from South Shields recording the installation of a water supply for the use of the garrison in AD 222 (or more accurately its renovation or enlargement, for the fort was already supplied by an aqueduct). In the third line, part of the emperor Severus Alexander's name has been erased following his murder and the condemnation of his name.

the study of fortresses which lie beneath cities such as Lincoln, Gloucester, Colchester, Exeter, Chester and York, much of their interiors being probably forever beyond the reach of excavation. At Colchester the plan of the fortress was divided into a series of strips across its width which were 200 and 300 Roman feet (*pes monetalis* = 0.295m) deep. Intensive work on the fragmentary plan at Exeter has shown how complicated the detailed surveying of the fortress was likely to have been (**16**). The overall scheme deduced from the excavation of limited areas may require modification in the future, but it provides a model which can be tested against new discoveries, often represented by small fragments of building plans recovered by restricted excavations or observed in modern service trenches.

The size of forts and their and garrisons

The long-term development of forts from the Republic down to the late Roman period resulted from changes in the structure and function of the Roman army. In Britain the size and garrisons of forts and fortresses were influenced in the shorter term mainly by the course of the conquest and the need to develop systems of frontier control. Many forts of the pre-Flavian period, the first twenty-five years of the conquest, are known in southern Britain, but only four – Nanstallon, Waddon Hill, Hod Hill and The Lunt, Baginton – have been excavated on an extensive scale. Hod Hill is the earliest and largest of these forts (4ha or 9.6 acres); its plan suggests that it contained a mixed garrison of legionaries and auxiliaries. The plans of the other three forts are fragmentary but what is known of the buildings at Nanstallon suggests that it was built for a part-mounted

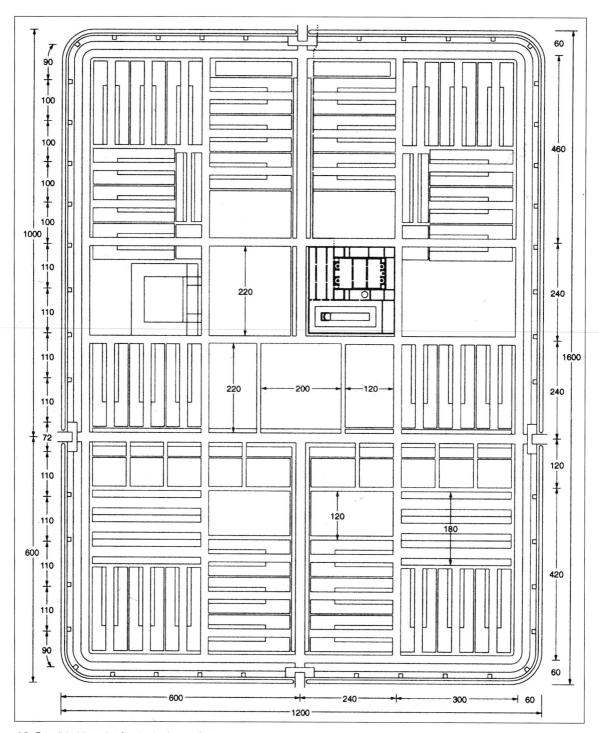

16 Possible blueprint for the legionary fortress
at Exeter. Dimensions are given in Roman feet
(1 Roman foot = 0.295m).

cohort (*cohors quingenaria equitata*). In the second century a unit of this type required a fort twice as large as Nanstallon (cf. Wallsend, described above); there was a tendency towards smaller forts in the conquest period.

Further evidence for mixed garrisons are 'vexillation fortresses' which at 8–12ha (20–30 acres) in area are several times larger than auxiliary forts but are too small to hold an entire legion (17). Longthorpe is the only example where significant details of the plan have been recovered: accommodation was apparently provided for 1,440 or perhaps 1,760 legionaries and about 1,000 auxiliaries including cavalry. Other such fortresses may have accommodated legionary vexillations or a number of auxiliary regiments brigaded together. Whatever forces they contained, these fortresses were for special groupings which cut across the regimental arrangements of the Roman army. They show the need for a number of points where large forces were concentrated and contrast with the familiar pattern of the second century, when fortresses contained whole legions and a large number of forts were provided for individual auxiliary units.

Nevertheless, in the pre-Flavian period legions were provided with fortresses capable of accommodating their full strength, even though large parts of a legion might actually be posted elsewhere for much of the time. The fortress at Colchester, established a year or so after the invasion in AD 43, was 20ha (49 acres) in area and was probably occupied by the Twentieth Legion; during the early years it was also the centre of Roman government in the new province. No other fortresses capable of holding a full legion are yet known for the years immediately following the invasion, and the other three legions were probably divided between a number of bases, as in the case of the Second Legion which may have been split between bases at Lake and Dorchester. After a decade or so, however, fortresses were provided for whole legions at Exeter, Kingsholm (Gloucester), Usk, Lincoln and Wroxeter (though not all were in occupation at the same time).

The early Flavian period saw the beginning of an advance into northern Britain which was to culminate in the occupation of Scotland south and east of the Highlands under the governor Agricola from AD 78/79 onwards. Three forts of this period in Scotland, at Fendoch, Strageath and Elginhaugh (18), have yielded almost complete plans. The details of Strageath and Elginhaugh suggest that they each contained more than one unit. However, at Inchtuthil a fortress planned to hold an entire legion was planted boldly in an advanced position. Although it was abandoned before completion, its excavation by Sir Ian Richmond has provided us with the best-understood plan of a fortress anywhere in the Roman Empire.

Forts of the Trajanic and Hadrianic periods, where sufficient is known of their plans, seem to have been built for single units. The most thoroughly explored example of this period is Wallsend (described above). Circumstances had changed by the early second century: Wales had long since been conquered but required a network of permanent garrisons to control it, while a northern limit to the province was fixed when the building of Hadrian's Wall began in the early AD 120s. These settled arrangements called for large numbers of forts containing single units, each supervising specific areas or lengths of the frontier. This was a matter of expediency and, when twenty years later the Antonine Wall was built, it included seventeen closely spaced forts along its length, some too small to hold complete units. In the early third century a vexillation fortress was built at Carpow during the Severan campaigns in Scotland and smaller legionary vexillations were placed in work compounds at Corbridge. By the end of that century new types of forts and units had appeared in Britain; these are described in Chapter 7.

Forts in systems of control and surveillance

Forts served many purposes but in most instances their positions were determined by the

17 A Roman military landscape at Water Eaton, Staffordshire. The location is important, for Watling Street, the road from London to the first-century legionary fortress at Wroxeter, forms a junction nearby with three other roads going to Chester, Metchley and Greensforge. The vexillation fortress is perhaps earliest in the sequence of military sites; there are two forts, presumably later than the vexillation fortress but both probably of first-century date, and no less than five temporary camps. *Pennocrucium*, which straddles Watling Street, is a settlement dating from the second century; the defences are later in date.

904   905

River Penk

Camp 1

Vexillation Fortress

Water Eaton
Coppice

Camp 2

111

Water Eaton

110

Water Eaton Lane

Watling Street

A 5

Pennocrucium

Eaton House

Fort

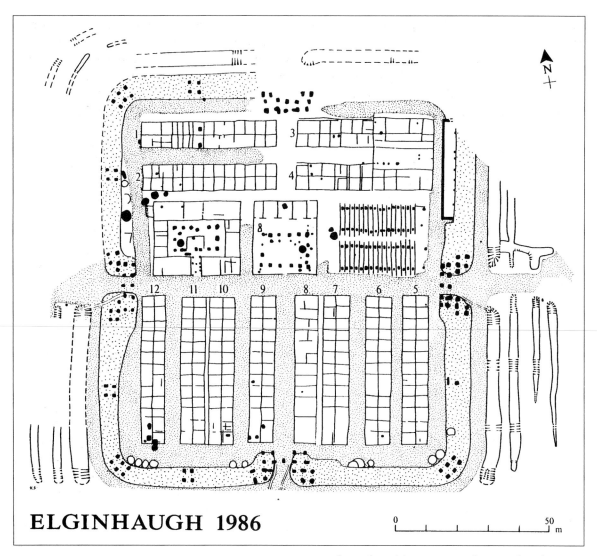

ELGINHAUGH 1986

0   50 m

18 Elginhaugh, a timber fort of 1.6ha (4 acres), which was occupied *c*. AD 80–6; the main excavations took place in 1986. The central range has a headquarters building, two granaries to the east and the commanding officer's house to the west. There are twelve other buildings in the fort, in addition to a building with stone footings set into the rear of the east rampart and which seems to have served as a workshop. Buildings 7 and 9–12 have ten *contubernia* and the less regular arrangements at the southern ends represent officers' houses. The plans of the remaining buildings are irregular in detail and this makes it difficult to identify their functions.

part they played in systems of control and surveillance. Campaigning armies built marching camps where the tents of the various units were set within an enclosure defended by a ditch and bank which could be formed in a few hours. Only rarely were attacks into new territory associated with more substantial construction: an example is at Richborough, site of a beach-head camp for the army of invasion (or part of it) in AD 43, which consisted of two parallel ditches and a rampart isolating a section of the shore. At a later stage forts were established to control newly conquered territory. Their disposition depended on the physical geography of the area and more particularly on the social and political structures of the subject peoples.

Having landed at Richborough the Roman army pushed westwards, defeating the Britons at the River Medway. The objective was now the *oppidum* of Camulodunum at Colchester, the capital of the Catuvellauni and the centre of resistance in south-east Britain. Within a few months matters had progressed sufficiently for the emperor Claudius to travel to Britain where he received the submission of eleven kings. In these early years of conquest the pattern of military occupation differed from what was to follow. For many years there had been treaties between the tribes of south-east Britain and Rome, and there was regular trade with Gaul. Rulers maintained effective control of their populations. If Rome could defeat or gain the allegiance of these rulers, it was easy enough to replace native rule by Roman authority. This is reflected by the disposition of forts. Colchester was at first the centre of the Roman administration and a fortress was planted in the pre-Roman *oppidum of Camulodunum*, a large settlement enclosed by a series of dykes 24km (15 miles) in length (**19**). The fortress was sited on previously unoccupied land near an area that seems to have been the industrial and commercial centre of the *oppidum*. A small enclosure 3.75km (2.3 miles) south-east of the fortress at Gosbecks seems to have been the royal compound. Nearby was a fort of 2.2ha (5.4 acres) which was large enough to accommodate an *ala*; its immediate purpose was perhaps to supervise the old focus of the *oppidum* which remained important as a religious centre throughout the Roman period.

The positioning of the military sites at Colchester is part of a pattern repeated throughout south-east Britain and in some adjacent areas. There are forts on or near important pre-Roman centres of population at Verulamium, Canterbury, Chichester, Winchester, Dorchester (near Maiden Castle), Dorchester-on-Thames, Cirencester (near the pre-Roman settlement of Bagendon) and

Leicester. Recently Silchester has been claimed as the site of a fortress. These were all large lowland settlements and without exception were to become Roman towns. Forts were also established inside Iron Age hillforts, as at Hod Hill, Maiden Castle, Hembury and Brandon Camp. These massive and very ancient fortifications had been tribal centres, even though some were only perhaps of symbolic importance by the time of the conquest, as at Hembury where there is no evidence of late Iron Age occupation.

By AD 47 the Roman army had advanced into the West Country, into the Welsh borders and as far north as the Humber. This marked a new stage in the conquest, for the army was beginning to enter more thinly populated areas where natural lines of communication were more difficult. There were few major settlements and it is usually supposed that the structure of native societies was less homogeneous than in south-east Britain. This required a network of forts spaced about 20km (12 miles – a day's march) apart which could be used to control large areas of land. Forts were usually built on virgin sites, often commanding a river crossing or junction of routes. Where there was a dispersed population, it was important to control lines of communication and many forts were sited on or near the Fosse Way, which ran for over 400km (250 miles) from east Devon to Lincoln and on to the Humber. For many years this road has been regarded as a frontier line marking the limit reached in the early years of conquest. This is doubtful, for some of the few forts in its vicinity which can be dated are Neronian. It seems more likely that the Fosse Way passed through a zone which was conquered and occupied piecemeal.

The late AD 40s and the AD 50s saw advances into Wales and the annexation of Devon and Cornwall. Even some thirty years ago it was still often maintained that there had been little significant military activity in the south-western peninsula. The discovery of a fortress at Exeter and of a number of forts in Devon has

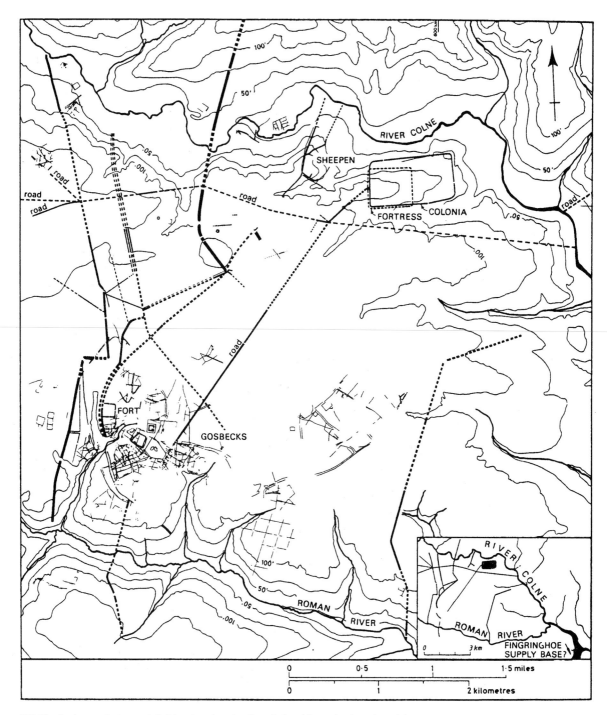

19 The legionary fortress at Colchester showing its relationship to the Iron Age dyke
systems (shown as heavy black lines) and settlements. Sheepen was the industrial and
commercial centre of the pre-Roman complex. The legionary fortress was built just to
the west of Sheepen which continued until AD 60 as an industrial area serving the army.
The focus of the Iron Age complex was at Gosbecks where there was an early Roman
fort, probably for cavalry. A temple and theatre were later built in this area.

completely changed the picture. The site for the fortress of the Second Legion was chosen not because it controlled a centre of pre-Roman power (as at Colchester) but because of military and logistical considerations. It overlooked the lowest bridgeable point on the River Exe, a few miles above its estuary, and had good inland communications with central Devon, west Devon and Cornwall; to the east an extension linked the fortress with the Fosse Way. A few years after the construction of the timber fortress in c. AD 55–60, the need for a legion based in the south-west seemed likely to last long enough to justify building baths in stone on an appropriately large scale (**colour plate 1**). The discovery of eight forts in Devon, entirely as a result of aerial photography, shows that a large force was required to control this newly conquered territory.

By the early AD 70s Roman control extended into northern Britain. A fort had been established at Carlisle and it is possible that other forts were established in south-west Scotland at the same time. The conquest of Scotland up to the edge of the Highlands took place later, during the governorship of Agricola (AD 77/8–83/4); his biography, written by his son-in-law Tacitus, supplies some details of the campaigns. This first occupation was short-lived (by the middle of AD 88 at the latest only forts south of the Forth–Clyde line were still held) with the result that the disposition of the forts is much clearer than in southern Britain. South of the Forth–Clyde isthmus, forts were concentrated along the roads leading north, with some outliers. To the north forts extended along a road running towards Stracathro; north-west of the road was a further series of forts controlling the mouths of the glens and thus blocking the natural routes through the Highlands. Some or all of these more northerly forts were built on the orders of Agricola's successor as governor, who was also responsible for building the fortress at Inchtuthil, abandoned before completion. At some stage in the first occupation of Scotland a chain of watch

towers was built along a road from south of Ardoch to Bertha. Each tower was founded on four posts within a circular enclosure formed by a bank and ditch. They were spaced less than a mile (1.6km) apart and their primary purpose was to ensure that there was no unauthorized passage across the line which they controlled. This is the first occurrence in Britain – and one of the earliest in the Empire as a whole – of an artificial frontier placed under permanent surveillance. At a slightly later date in Germany much longer systems of watch towers were built, to which wooden palisades and ditches were added. Forts were integral parts of such systems, supplying men for duty at the watch towers and for patrols along the frontier line; they also provided the larger forces needed to deal with serious threats to the frontier.

Following the abandonment of gains beyond the Forth–Clyde isthmus in the late AD 80s, much of lowland Scotland remained in occupation. However, further forts had been given up by AD 105 and the Stanegate, a road covering much of the distance between the Tyne and the Solway, became an important element of the frontier zone. Forts were spaced less than 7 miles (11km) apart along its length from Corbridge to the Solway and at some stage small forts (less than 0.4ha or 1 acre in size) were introduced in at least two places between the larger forts. Although there were also isolated watch towers, this system of forts cannot be regarded as a frontier of the type seen on the Gask Ridge. However, in the AD 120s the emperor Hadrian recognized the need for an artificial barrier and ordered the construction of what was to become the most elaborate and best known of all Roman frontier works (**20** and **colour plate 2**).

Hadrian's Wall, as originally planned and partly built, consisted of a wall made of stone for about two-thirds of its length from its eastern terminus and of turf to the west, with fortlets (milecastles) at intervals of about a mile and two towers (turrets) between each milecastle. The Stanegate forts between Carlisle

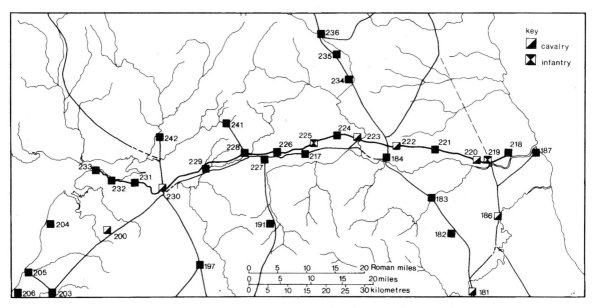

20 Hadrian's Wall (for key to numbers see p.13). Units shown as in the third century; solid black squares represent mixed units of mounted and foot soldiers.

and Corbridge lay only a short distance to the south of the Wall, and at first it was decided not to place forts on the line of the Wall. However, this decision was soon reversed and forts were built at intervals of about seven or eight miles (11–13km), with two forts at larger intervals. Further modifications were made to the scheme and there were eventually fifteen forts on the Wall; in addition the forts on the Stanegate at Corbridge and Vindolanda remained in use.

Each fort was allocated a section of the Wall, and probably provided soldiers for patrolling and to man the milecastles and turrets. The territory beyond the Wall would also require supervision and the outpost forts beyond the western part of the Wall at Birrens, Netherby and Bewcastle were certainly occupied under Hadrian. High Rochester and Risingham, which controlled the main route into Scotland, are probably also of this period, even though the limited excavations have recovered no firm evidence of Hadrianic occupation. By the time the whole Wall system was completed, as much as a third of all the non-legionary troops in Britain were stationed in the Wall zone.

The identity of many of the original garrisons of the Wall-forts is unknown, but most of the third-century garrisons are known from inscriptions and other evidence; these probably represent a balance of forces similar to that in the second century. Cavalry was present in strength, with a milliary *ala* (the only unit of that size in Britain) at Stanwix, and three *alae quingenariae* in forts along the eastern part of the Wall; in addition there were *alae* at Old Carlisle and Chester-le-Street, within easy reach of the Wall. The remaining garrisons that are known were part-mounted with the exception of Newcastle, Housesteads and Birdoswald where there were only foot soldiers. The reasons for the deployment of troops in the forts of the Wall zone are clear enough. The cavalry units were placed as near as possible to roads running north of the Wall (a road running north from Newcastle is probable but not proven), so that a large force could be moved rapidly beyond the Wall to reinforce the outpost forts. Furthermore, with the exception of Chesters the cavalry forts lie within the coastal plains or the gently undulating country that overlooks the plains. In these areas cavalry could operate to best effect. The inclusion in the frontier forces of six of the ten or eleven cavalry units in Britain emphasizes the importance that was attached to a rapid and

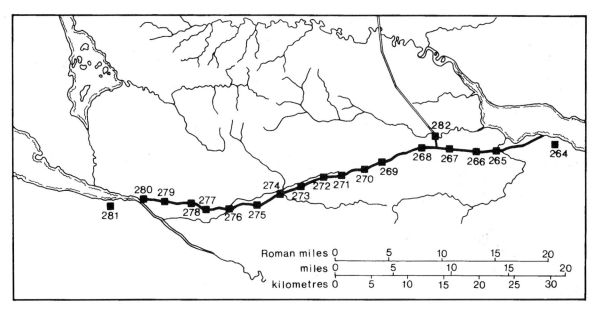

aggressive response to any threat to the Wall.

In c. AD 140 Hadrian's Wall was abandoned and the Antonine Wall was built on the Forth–Clyde isthmus (**21**). As in the case of its predecessor, the original plan was modified, the result being a dense concentration of forts along its line. A spacing of forts at intervals of 2–3 miles (3–5km) along its length of 37 miles (60km) seems to have been intended, as compared with the spacing of 6–7 miles (10–11km) common to most of the forts on Hadrian's Wall. This new line eventually proved impossible to hold and in the AD 160s Hadrian's Wall was recommissioned.

With one or two exceptions in Wales, the forts garrisoned after the abandonment of the Antonine Wall were held until the fourth century, and the majority until the end of the Roman period. In 1969 A. L. F. Rivet described them as 'unsuccessful forts': their enduring presence was a symbol of Rome's failure to absorb the areas they controlled into the mainstream of ordinary provincial life. The later history of these forts is discussed in Chapter 7.

Specialized uses of forts

In the preceding section the use of forts during the conquest period and in the consolidation of frontiers has been described. Some forts served

21 The Antonine Wall (for key to numbers see p. 13).

more specialized purposes concerned with the control of industrial activities, military logistics and the needs of government.

In the second and third centuries the fort of Caernarvon in North Wales contained, in addition to the commander's house in its usual position next to the headquarters building, another larger residence with its own baths, which was probably for an imperial procurator overseeing mineral extraction in the region, particularly lead mining. Other forts concerned with mining are known at Whitley Castle and Charterhouse; in addition, the *classis Britannica* was engaged in extensive ironworking in the Sussex Weald. Criminals were often condemned to work in the mines, and these forts were perhaps also responsible for penal settlements.

An army on campaign is dependent on its supply lines, apart from what it can gain by foraging or capture. Coastal supply bases connected with the Claudian campaigns are known at Richborough and Fishbourne and are suspected at other sites. They were principally intended for the storage of grain, particularly wheat, which was as vital to the functioning of an ancient army as fuel oil is to a modern army. At Llanfor in North Wales, a large fort, probably

41

of late Claudian or Neronian date and some 3.6ha (8.9 acres) in area, lies next to a supply base which consists of a five-sided enclosure with two gates in its longest side. A Severan and later Roman supply base at South Shields is discussed in Chapter 6. To the same general period belong the two legionary compounds at Corbridge (**colour plate 3**). These were enclosures walled off from the surrounding town, which contained headquarters buildings, barracks and workshops. The legionaries stationed there might have performed financial, administrative and police duties in the frontier area. There are indications of similar compounds in the Roman town at Carlisle, and the town at Aldborough has produced enough military equipment of second- and third-century date to make the presence of a military garrison probable (**22**).

The large fort (4.5ha or 11 acres) at Cripplegate in London served as a base for the many soldiers engaged in government duties in the capital and perhaps also in policing this largest of all the cities in Roman Britain.

The Saxon Shore forts

No better example can be found of the difficulties in determining the tactical and strategic use of forts than the problem of the Saxon Shore. This was the term employed to describe the command of the count in charge of a series of forts along the coast of Britain, from the Solent to the Wash. We know of this official post only from the *Notitia Dignitatum*, a late Roman list of offices. Until recently there had been no disagreement about the function and origins of the forts under the count's command (which at some date before the compilation of the *Notitia Dignitatum* had also included a series of forts on the other side of the Channel). Towards the end of the third century seaborne attacks by Saxon and Frankish raiders threatened the security of Britain. To prevent these attacks eight forts built in the massive style of the period (described in Chapter 3) were combined with two existing forts to provide a system of garrisons and naval harbours (none of the latter has been explored). Together with the forts on the other side of the Channel they formed a zone of maritime control which

22 Military equipment from the Roman town of Aldborough. This is evidence for a Roman garrison in the town, perhaps accommodated in a compound as at Corbridge. These fittings come from baldrics (sword belts); they incorporate the motto 'OPTIME MAXIME CON(SERVA) NVMERVUM OMNIVM MILITANTIVM' ('Best and Greatest [i.e. Jupiter], preserve the number of all those serving'), to be read in the openwork decoration of several adjacent mounts on the belts. The letters surrounding the eagle mount have broken away, but one mount (centre) preserves the letters 'MI...TIUM' and another (right) the word 'OMNIUM'.

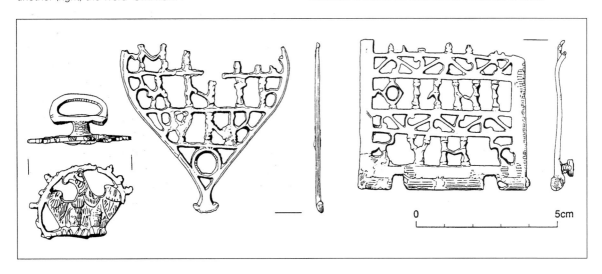

blocked the approaches to the north-west flank of the Roman Empire. Small raiding parties which eluded naval patrols could be quickly mopped up by the shore-based troops.

These arguments for a grand military design have recently been questioned. The literary evidence for Saxon and Frankish raiding is unsatisfactory; and, perhaps more tellingly, recent research has suggested that Germanic peoples, who used large open rowing boats, would have faced journeys of impossibly long duration to reach Britain: for example, in the best conditions and with perfect navigation, it would have taken eleven days hugging the coast and a sea-crossing of twenty-four hours to reach East Anglia from Jutland. When Anglo-Saxon raiding and migration began in the fifth century, it was launched from settlements by then established along the coast of northern Gaul. The Saxon Shore forts, rather than being part of a defensive system, were intended to support inland garrisons and assist in the exploitation of natural and agricultural resources in Britain. They perhaps also served as holding camps for troops in transit, especially perhaps the field army in Gaul which might have been needed to deal with large-scale warfare in Britain. In other words they were little more than fortified ports, essential links in the logistical system but with no major part to play in maritime or coastal defence.

This new perspective on the function of the Saxon Shore forts has its own weaknesses. Just because the literary sources are silent, we cannot safely assume that Britain was secure from external threats. The journeys by raiders would have been feasible if they had rested in deserted coves and inlets along the Gaulish coast, unless we assume that there was immediate Roman supervision and control of every mile of the coastline. Attacks might also have been anticipated from the North: the tribes beyond the Wall posed serious problems for the Roman

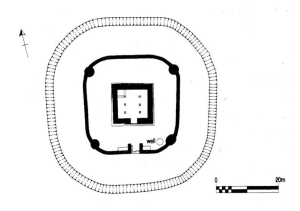

23 The late Roman signal station at Goldsborough, consisting of a central tower and a walled enclosure defended by a ditch. The discovery of regularly-spaced hearths between the tower and east wall, not recorded on plan, suggests the presence of small barracks, perhaps of timber and thus missed by the excavators.

army in the fourth century, if not before. Towards the end of the fourth century, attacks by sea led to the construction of a series of large defended posts along the Yorkshire coast (**23**); whether this was a response to a new threat, or a desperate attempt, involving the only major later fourth-century addition to the military defences of Britain, to deal with a long-standing problem, is impossible to determine.

Recent excavations by Professor M. Fulford at Pevensey have now revived a view first promulgated by D. A. White almost forty years ago. Coins and dendrochronology combine to show that the fort was built during the reigns of the usurping emperors Carausius and Allectus (AD 286–96), whose centre of power was Britain. It now seems likely that the Saxon Shore forts, excluding the earlier forts at Reculver and Brancaster, were built as a defence against the emperor Maximian rather than against barbarian raiders. The question of their purpose once Britain was joined again with the rest of the Empire remains unanswered.

3
Defence of the Empire

Military threats and civil disorder

Until the late third century the defences of Roman forts were not devised to withstand attacks by large, well-equipped bodies of men, nor did they include any features to counteract siege machinery. No special care was taken to build them on strongly defensible sites, and sometimes the positions chosen were very weak indeed, as at Exeter where attacking forces could have overlooked the legionary fortress from the volcanic knoll of Rougemont. The first two centuries of Roman occupation in Britain saw the army at the height of its achievement. Major attacks would have been dealt with in the field, good communications and intelligence ensuring that adequate forces were assembled in good time. Of course, things could and did go wrong. In AD 60/61 the rebels led by Boudica carried all before them, and in *c.* AD 180 tribes from the North crossed a 'Wall', probably Hadrian's Wall, and killed a general, either a legionary legate or possibly the governor himself. Nevertheless, large-scale attacks seem to have been regarded as a contingency too remote to influence the design of fort defences.

There were certainly threats of a less overwhelming nature. In the military areas, raiding from beyond the frontiers – and perhaps even from remoter areas within the frontiers – was probably always a problem. A third-century tombstone from Ambleside, recording the names of two soldiers '*in cast(ris) inte(rfectus) ab hosti(bus)*' ('killed in the fort by the enemy') shows at the very least that such outbreaks could have serious consequences (although the use of the word '*hostes*' might suggest that the fort had been carried by something more formidable than a raiding party). Retaliation or pre-emptive actions by the Roman army were commemorated by a dedication to Hercules at Carlisle and to an unknown deity at Corbridge (**24**). Brigandage and piracy might have occurred at times in Britain; in some parts of the Empire they were endemic. Above all, the policing function of the army in the military zones, enforcing laws and assisting in the collection of taxes, hardly made it a popular institution, especially as soldiers often treated civilians with casual brutality. A writing-tablet from Vindolanda contains an appeal for justice from a foreigner, probably a trader, who had been badly beaten with sticks.

Apart from their defensive function, the ditches, walls, gates and towers which enclosed forts made a firm statement about the presence and power of the Roman army. This was more than a matter of ostentation, for military law made it clear that the defences were a sacred boundary: illicit passage across them was a serious crime for soldiers as well as civilians.

Defences in turf and timber

A ditch in front of a bank formed from its upcast was dug to defend a unit camping overnight in hostile territory. The defences of forts in Britain until the end of the first century, and in some cases for a further century, were

LEG·A
Q·CALPVRN
CONCESZINI
VS·PRAEF·EQ
CAESA·CORI
ONOTOTAR
VM·MANVPR
AÉSENTISSIMI
NVMINIS·DÉVS

24 Altar from Corbridge found in the crypt of Hexham Abbey and now lost. It recorded the slaughter of a band of Corionototae (*caesa Corionototarum manu*) by a prefect of cavalry; the Corionototae were an otherwise unknown Northern British people, probably a sub-division of the Brigantes.

merely larger and more durable versions of these field defences, equipped with wooden gates and towers. Instead of a bank of piled earth, there was a rampart usually about 6m (20ft) in width, its front and rear faces built of carefully laid turves or clay blocks which retained a core of material, usually spoil from the defensive ditch or ditches. Foundation platforms of rubble, cobbles or timber were sometimes provided, and some ramparts were laced with horizontal timbers at intervals. On occasions, box-ramparts, with revetments of timber rather than turf or clay, have been encountered.

Most excavations in forts, no matter how small in scale, have usually included at least one trench through the defences, which in the case of turf and timber forts will usually be the only indication of their presence visible from the ground. In recent years, large areas of defences have been stripped, thereby yielding more comprehensive and reliable information about their construction. However, preservation of ramparts as more than denuded earthworks only occurs when they have been encased in the larger ramparts associated with the addition of stone walls. At Chester paving thought to represent the rampart walk was found at a height of about 2m (6ft), and at Lincoln the rampart survives nowhere higher than 2.5m (8ft). Caesar mentions ramparts 10 and 12 Roman feet (3.0 and 3.6m) in height: it is surprising to find ramparts much lower in height at these two legionary fortresses.

Even in the rare instances of ramparts preserved at their full heights, there are many questions which excavation alone cannot answer: for example, how much labour did their construction require, what skills did the work force need, and what maintenance was required after their construction? Some answers have been supplied by experimental reconstructions at Vindolanda, Metchley and The Lunt, Baginton. The lengths of rampart built at The Lunt in 1966 and 1970, which are still standing, have been particularly informative (**25**). Both were built to the same dimensions with a width of 5.4m (18ft) and a height of 3.6m (12ft). Allowing for the slope of the front and rear faces, the rampart walk was just under 2m (6ft) in width. The rampart built in 1966 had cheeks of turves, cut to a standard size and laid grass to grass and earth to earth, which retained a core of earth with a width one-third that of the rampart. After eight years the rampart was still in good condition and, despite burrowing by badgers, needed no repair. Silting had to be cleared from the ditch every spring, and erosion gradually changed its profile from a sharp V to a U-shape. The turves in the length of rampart built in 1970 were laid with the grass downwards, which prevented marked settling that had occurred in the earlier rampart.

25 Rear view of reconstructed turf rampart and timber gate at The Lunt, Baginton. Note the gap between the top of the rampart and the timber breastwork, caused by the settling of the turf facings and earth core of the rampart.

In addition to the ramparts there were timber towers and gates. The plans of the towers were square or rectangular and were represented by four or six posts. Much more variation occurred in the plans of gates: they might have one or two carriageways, and towers above the carriageways or flanking them (**26**). Sometimes they took an elaborate form, as at Carlisle where the south gate of the fort was remarkably well preserved. The timber-laced rampart which led to the discovery of the fort was first seen in 1973, and the gate was excavated in 1978 and in the course of the 1980s. It had two carriageways flanked by towers. The front of the carriageways was set back behind the line of the rampart, the ends of which were revetted with vertical timber planks, forming a vantage-court which could be commanded from above the carriageways and from the two flanking towers which extended above the ends of the rampart. The timber which had formed the threshold of the carriageways survived in position (it is now displayed in the Tullie House Museum, Carlisle). It is an oak beam 6.6m (21.6ft) in length and 200mm (8in) thick with holes for the pivots of the gates, each of which were of two leaves; the western

In 1966 between seven and ten men worked on the reconstruction for twenty days, on average for six hours a day. At that rate 300 men working a longer ten-hour day could have completed the entire circuit of the fort rampart in between nine and twelve days in ideal weather conditions. The work required no particular skills, although a high degree of coordination would no doubt have been needed if 300 men were working on the defences at the same time.

Experimental work of this kind is of great value. Although there will always be quibbles over details, the information from The Lunt can be used to make broad estimates of the effort required in the construction of the many forts and fortresses with turf defences in Britain. It also provides a yardstick against which to measure claims such as those of Caesar that the Nervii built 3 miles (5km) of defences in three hours.

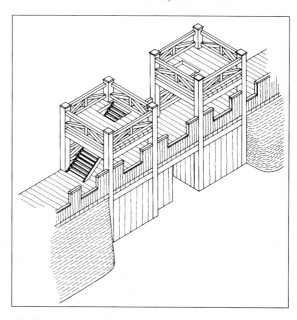

26 Timber gate with a single carriageway; a conjectural reconstruction of the east gate at Buckton.

carriageway had seen more use than the eastern, as was evident from deep cartwheel ruts spaced 1.60m (5ft) apart on the surface of the beam (27). The two towers above the ends of the rampart extended to the rear to flank the carriageways, forming small rooms at ground level; access to these rooms was only possible from the first floor. From ground level the rampart walk and the upper storeys of the gate were reached by an *ascensus*, a stairway represented by a platform of turf built against the base of the rampart.

Defences built in stone

About fifty years after the conquest of Britain, the Roman army began to build defences in stone rather than in turf and timber. The earliest instance of this is at Inchtuthil where the defences were being rebuilt in stone when the legionary fortress was abandoned in *c.* AD 86. Some twenty years or so were to elapse before fort defences also began to be built in stone. By the Hadrianic period the use of stone was normal, although there were exceptions such as all but two of the forts on the Antonine Wall; the latest occurrence of defences in turf and timber is the early third-century fortress at Carpow.

The state of preservation of the defences at Birdoswald (**colour plate 4**), Housesteads, Chesters and High Rochester is almost

27 Oak beam forming the threshold of the south gate of the Flavian fort at Carlisle. The double-leaved gate closed against the central door stop (behind ranging pole); wear from cart wheels is visible on the right-hand part of the threshold.

unrivalled among auxiliary forts in the European provinces, but many questions still remain to be answered about the form of the gates, interval towers and walls. Considerable advances have been made recently, resulting in particular from the analysis of standing remains.

Until the later third century, defences in stone were of simple form. The curtain walls were usually 1.2–1.5m (4–5ft) in width and probably 3.6–4.5m (12–15ft) in height to the level of the wall walk. At the rear of the wall was an earth bank which rose to the level of the wall walk. It is sometimes claimed that the bank was lower than the wall walk but this has never been established beyond doubt and is unlikely, for the purpose of the bank, in addition to strengthening the wall, was to extend the width of the wall walk, providing a serviceable fighting platform. Towers stood at the angles of the walls and were inserted at regular intervals between the gates and angle-towers.

Forts and fortresses alike were almost always provided with four gates. Exceptions occur on

47

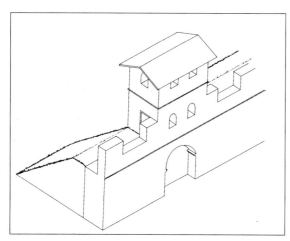

28 Conjectural reconstruction of the west gate of Stone Fort 1 at Vindolanda, probably built in AD 122–4. Its construction seems to have preceded the decision to build forts on Hadrian's Wall, which were equipped with much larger gates (see **29**).

Hadrian's Wall in forts which project by about a third of their length beyond the Wall; three gates with double carriageways were provided beyond the Wall and three behind, the two on the long sides having single carriageways with a tower above. Gates in the Trajanic–Hadrianic period were otherwise usually of a standard plan: two carriageways with arched openings to front and rear were flanked by towers, the fronts of which were flush with the curtain wall (**29**). The carriageways had two-leaved wooden gates on pivots which closed against the inner side of the front arched opening. The well-preserved bases of gate towers, the piers from which the arches sprang and the pivots for the gates can all be seen at Chesters, Housesteads, Great Chesters and Birdoswald (see **colour plate 4**).

During the course of the second and third centuries the design of gates underwent some changes. A defensive modification was the substitution of single for double carriageways, as is seen in all the gates of forts on the Antonine Wall. The walling-up of one of the double carriageways of fort gates on Hadrian's Wall at an early stage shows that they were unnecessary. Later instances of double

carriageways are known, as for example at South Shields which was built in the AD 160s (**colour plate 5**). They were still used when a striving after architectural effect was placed before utility. Indeed, it was probably more the desire to make fort gates more imposing than improvements in their defensibility that explains changes in their design after the Hadrianic period. City gates of the earlier Roman period were often of great size and elaboration, and it is understandable that the design of fort gates should eventually exceed what was required in strictly military terms. Gates were where the main dedicatory inscriptions were placed, proclaiming the name of the emperor whose purposes the fort was built to serve. As the point of departure or return in any journey, whether warlike or peaceful, gates might be expected to play an important part in military ceremonial or ritual. That is certainly hinted at by an account of the emperor Valentinian who feared the worst when he could not depart for a campaign in Gaul from the same gate by which he had entered a city because the iron-clad gate-leaf was stuck; his forebodings were justified, for he died of apoplexy shortly afterwards. Just as in the British navy of the eighteenth and nineteenth centuries, when a captain or senior officer

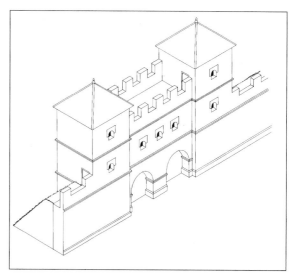

29 Conjectural reconstruction of one of the Hadrianic gates at Housesteads.

coming to the starboard side of a ship had to be piped aboard and greeted by an honour guard yet could board to larboard without any formalities, so might the various gates of a Roman fort have been used according to particular circumstances – the *porta praetoria*, for example, being reserved for ceremonial entrances.

Signs of elaboration emerge early in the history of stone fort gates. In Germany during the Flavian period, the towers were built to project as little as 0.2–0.3m (8–12in) beyond the face of the fort wall. This could have served no conceivable military purpose and was meant to emphasize visually the façade of the gate. Gate towers projecting by up to 2m (6ft) occur in Britain from the mid-second century onwards, as at South Shields (see **colour plate 5**) and Brecon Gaer. Once again, this was to achieve an architectural effect; if the towers had been built to project to increase their defensibility, there would also have been projecting interval and corner towers so that the walls could have been protected by lateral enfilading fire from the sides of the towers, as in late Roman systems of fortification. At Castell Collen in the mid-second century and at Risingham (**30**) in the early third century, gate towers were built with semi-circular fronts (or at Risingham more accurately with a seven-sided front). They probably resembled the late second-century *porta praetoria* of the legionary fortress at Regensburg in southern Germany; this gate, which survives in part to the top of its second storey, was decorated with an elaborately moulded string course, and the façade of its surviving tower was pierced at first-floor level by large, closely spaced windows.

Unfortunately, very few fragments of masonry with architectural ornament can be associated with gates in Britain, but the meagre record nevertheless suggests that some were highly decorated and were not as austerely utilitarian as is often supposed. There are blocks with dentils (a horizontal line of evenly spaced cubical projections) from Birdoswald and Old

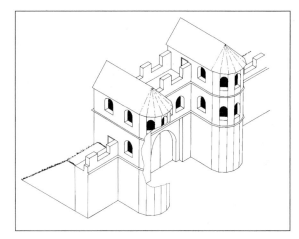

30 Conjectural reconstruction of the south gate at Risingham.

Penrith, and elaborately moulded cornices can be associated with gates at Housesteads and Vindolanda (the west gate of Stone Fort 2, *c.* AD 223–5). Some sites such as Chesters and Vindolanda have produced small attached columns, and it is possible these also came from the façades of gates.

Beyond the walls were systems of defensive ditches. Generally V-shaped in section and rarely more than 2m (6ft) in depth, they were not formidable obstacles individually. But there were always at least two ditches and often more: beyond the west wall of Whitley Castle there were seven, on the north side of Birrens there were six and on the east side of Ardoch (**31**) there were five. These are isolated forts which needed extra protection but there are many others, such as South Shields and Old Penrith, with three or four ditches, an effective means of breaking up an assault and trapping the attackers in a field of fire.

Fort walls were usually built with a mortared rubble core and with small facing stones set in mortar; from the Hadrianic period onwards some were built with chamfered plinths at their base. At Birdoswald, Vindolanda, Great Chesters and elsewhere, repairs to the fort wall can be seen. Visitors admire the lichened stonework and its subtle weathered tones, but it is important to remember that Roman practice

31 View across four of the five defensive ditches on the east side of the fort at Ardoch; the causeway leads to the east gate.

was often to render such walls with white plaster, often picking out a scheme of false masonry-jointing in bright red paint. The fortress at Chester has the best-preserved stretches of defensive walls of any military site in Roman Britain. The walls on two sides were removed when the circuit of defences was enlarged in medieval times, but on the north and east sides substantial lengths survive to the height of a string course in the form of a moulding which marks the level of the wall walk. The masonry was of very large blocks some 0.3–0.34m (12–13in) in height and 1.2–1.6m (4–5¼ft) in length, laid without mortar as is usual in this technique of construction, which is known as *opus quadratum* (**32**). These lengths of walling have long been recognized as Roman, and excavations have proved that it was inserted in front of the original turf rampart of the fortress.

The date of the wall and the history of its repairs remain uncertain, but analysis of the fabric by Tim Strickland on behalf of Chester City Council has shown that the stretches where the string courses survive are of one build. The curious battering of the upper courses, taken in the past to signify a repair, has in fact resulted from the blocks slipping backwards as deposits behind the wall gradually compacted.

The forts of the Saxon Shore

The possible functions of the Saxon Shore forts has been discussed in the previous chapter. In any consideration of Roman fort defences they are of great importance: collectively, they represent the best-preserved late Roman examples in the western part of the Empire. The system incorporated forts at Reculver and Brancaster which had probably been built in the early third century, but the remaining eight forts were built later in the third century to designs which represent a radical departure from the simple defences of the preceding centuries. The rectangular plan was abandoned, and in some cases the forts were square or irregular with five or more sides; at Pevensey the walls described a rough oval. Their walls were up to 4m (13ft) thick and probably stood to a height of 7–8m (23–26ft). At frequent intervals there were towers which projected beyond the face of the wall (**colour plate 6**). At some forts the towers were part of the original construction; at others they were clearly secondary, although perhaps added during the building of the forts as a modification to the original design. The gates were all built with single carriageways but otherwise varied a great deal: some were flanked by projecting towers, and at Pevensey and Portchester the main gates were set behind the line of the walls so that the area in front of them could have been commanded by fire from three sides (**33**). Even the techniques of construction

differed from those of earlier forts. The foundations of the walls, of concrete or rammed chalk, were reinforced by wooden frameworks and sometimes underpinned by wooden piles. The walls, of flint or neatly squared stone, had horizontal tile courses at intervals, and the exterior faces were often pointed with a strong pink mortar containing an aggregate of crushed

32 The north wall of the legionary fortress at Chester. The wall was about 4.6m (15ft) in height from a chamfered plinth to the top of the moulded string course, here surviving in its original position. In places recent repairs have revealed above the string course a line of blocks with rounded edges at the front and rear with a slot cut in their upper surfaces. The slot was to accommodate a parapet wall which perhaps consisted of monolithic upright slabs forming merlons and embrasures.

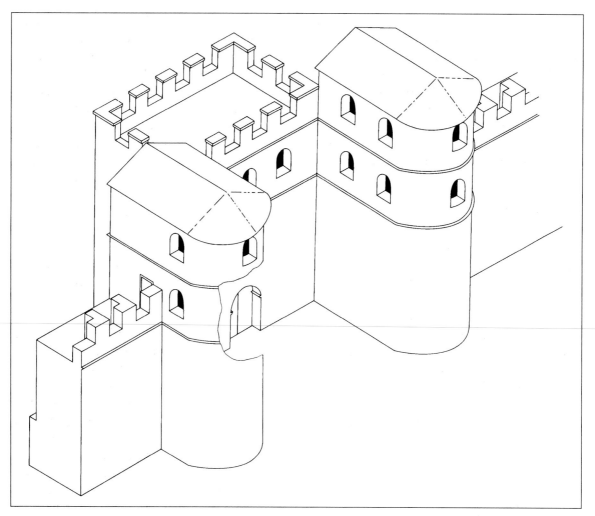

33 The main west gate at Pevensey; note the merlons with rearward projections to give defenders added protection (information from M. Lyne) and the absence of a rampart behind the wall.

brick. Two other forts of this type are known on the west coast of Britain, at Cardiff and Lancaster, and were no doubt meant to deal with raiders from Ireland.

No attempt was made to modernize existing forts by the addition of projecting towers, although the fortress at York had eight polygonal towers added to its south-east wall. The two great angle-towers were 15m (49ft) in width and one survives to a height of 6m (20ft). Across the River Ouse was the *colonia* of York, which was the capital city of *Britannia Inferior*,

the northern province created when Britain was divided into two provinces in the early third century. The river front of the fortress was embellished with towers to dominate the *colonia* which it overlooked; no towers were added to the other three sides to make the walls more defensible.

This style of fortification, although a novelty in Roman military architecture, had many antecedents in the ancient world, particularly in the defences of Hellenistic cities. It had been devised so that the defenders could use stone-throwing machines and catapults against substantial onslaughts. In the unsettled conditions of the later third century, many cities of the Roman Empire which had been undefended for centuries were now enclosed by strong walls and towers, and the army, with its engineers perhaps responsible for the design of the city walls, followed the current style of fortification when building new forts.

The forts of the Saxon Shore, and at Lancaster and Cardiff, were the last large-scale fortifications to be built by the Roman army in Britain. Existing forts and fortresses were repaired when necessary but the only new fortifications were minor coastal defences, such as the Yorkshire signal stations which were built in the last quarter of the fourth century.

Defences and weaponry

The form which the defences of forts took depended on the perception of threat. In the first and second centuries, and for well into the third century, defences were on a modest scale, reflecting the confidence of the army in its ability to repel any attack and then to pursue the enemy in the open. The lofty, thick walls and towers of the late coastal forts are eloquent of a more cautious view that anticipated determined attacks which might not be beaten off easily. The details of defensive systems demonstrate the use of different types of weapons. The merlons on early fort walls were widely spaced, which was necessary for the use of hand-thrown projectiles such as stones and javelins or throwing spears. Later walls have embrasures on average no wider than the merlons, which particularly suited archery. For the most part evidence for changes in the width of embrasures comes from outside Britain. However, solid stone lintels pierced with semi-

circular window heads from a number of forts on Hadrian's Wall show that the width of windows in towers and gates was very narrow, about two Roman feet (0.59m). This would seem to confine their use in defence to archers. The towers and gates of late Roman forts had much larger windows, as at Pevensey where a window survived in one of the towers until it was obliterated by the insertion of a machine-gun nest during the Second World War. Windows of this size were necessary for mechanical arrow- and stone-shooters.

Better understanding of how fort defences were planned depends on determining the range, accuracy and rate of delivery of missiles. Several reconstructions of mechanical arrow-shooters and stone-throwers have been attempted, which have certainly supported the claims of classical authors for their effectiveness. In the earlier Roman period these formidable weapons were mainly used in open battle, and were especially associated with the legions. Fort defences of the period were devised for the use of hand-thrown weapons. At South Shields the re-enactment society Quinta has used the reconstructed south-west gate and adjacent stretches of fort wall in a programme of research on these simple weapons (34). As in so many archaeological experiments, it did not prove possible to replicate exactly all the essentials: weapons were made to the correct specifications but the skills of their users were rudimentary,

34 Ranges of hand-thrown missiles as determined by experiments at South Shields; throwing stones reached ditch C, javelins ditch B.

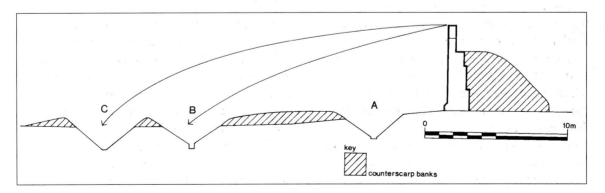

whereas their Roman counterparts would have had the benefit of frequent practice. Although the experiments could thus only establish the minimum effectiveness of these weapons, they yielded surprising results. Throwing stones by hand proved to be a very versatile and damaging method of defence. In northern Britain stones worked to a roughly spherical shape and weighing 0.5–1.0kg (1–2lb) are fairly common finds in forts; they often have a flattened facet to allow for easier stacking. From the walkway along the top of the fort wall at South Shields, at a height of 4m (13ft) above ground level, it proved possible to throw stones on average for a distance of 25m (27 yards), that is, as far as the outermost defensive ditch. Most impressive was the ability of the untrained participants to throw stones at intervals of two to three seconds with reasonable accuracy. The effects of a withering hail of these stones were easy to imagine.

The experiments with javelins or throwing spears yielded less spectacular results. The average range was 15–20m (16–22 yards) and it was difficult to achieve much accuracy. However, the rate of delivery was as fast as that of the throwing stones. Experiments were also made with slings. These can be whirled around in vertical circles at the side of the thrower, or in horizontal circles above the head. There was not enough room on the wall walk for the first method; the slinger, who was only moderately experienced, had not mastered the second method but doubted whether the space between the merlons was sufficient for its use.

Even within the limitations imposed by the lack of skill of the experimenters, it is easy to see how the ditch systems around forts were zones which attackers could scarcely hope to cross unscathed. Experienced soldiers could have maintained devastatingly accurate and rapid volleys, while the attackers, climbing in and out of the ditches and with no cover, had little chance of carrying the defences. The gates were weak points usually where solid causeways for the approach roads crossed the ditches. Archers stationed at the small windows in the gates and on their flat roofs would have had attackers well within range before they reached the causeways. The reconstructed gate at South Shields has twelve windows on its exterior side, as well as space for a further eight archers on the flat roof over the chamber above the carriageways. Against a determined well-organized attack, the defences of these first- and second-century forts would have been of less use. If archers and slingers provided cover for direct attempts on the walls, the short-range weapons of the defenders would have been difficult to employ. In Britain, however, there is no reason to think that the native peoples were proficient in the military use of archery or were capable of laying siege to a fort, and it was not until the late Roman period that forts defensible against large-scale attacks were built.

4
Palaces and hovels: buildings in the fort

Living space in forts

The interiors of forts and fortresses were largely occupied by accommodation for their garrisons. In legionary fortresses the legates lived in houses so large that they can justifiably be termed palaces; ordinary soldiers were packed into barracks where they lived in cramped conditions. The study of these buildings is potentially a rich source of information about the culture of the garrisons and their living conditions and social organization. The reasons why this potential has not been fully realized are varied. In timber forts and fortresses, unless they are sealed beneath later structures, all that can usually be recovered are the ground plans; floors have been destroyed by ploughing and finds displaced from their original contexts. On deeply stratified sites excavators in the past were often drawn to buildings such as the headquarters or granaries where the results obtainable would produce a seemingly clear-cut history of the fort or fortress, perhaps supported by the lucky find of a building inscription. When well-preserved barracks or officers' houses have been encountered, until recently they were usually trenched, an excavation technique too insensitive to recover much useful information.

Given that little more than outline plans have been available, it is hardly surprising that attention has focused on broad issues such as how many barracks a certain type of unit would require. In this chapter the emphasis is mainly on large-scale excavations which show that, if

all the evidence that lies in the ground can be recovered, much can be learnt about the everyday life of the officers and men.

Accommodation for senior officers

The legate who commanded a legion occupied a position of great power, subordinate only to the governor of the province, unless these offices were combined, as in the third century when the governor of *Britannia Inferior* (northern Britain) was also legate of the Sixth Legion at York. Officers of such high rank needed a magnificent residence. Only parts of the legates' palaces have been explored in the legionary fortresses of Britain but at Caerleon the excavated portion includes a long colonnaded area with semi-circular ends, a feature which also occurs in the legates' palaces of the double legionary fortress of Vetera in Germany. These areas were perhaps laid out as gardens and the surrounding colonnades might have been the settings for many important decisions taken in the course of pleasant strolls, a reminder that the sedentary meeting is very much a modern way of transacting business. The estimated size of the Caerleon palace far exceeds the area of the largest houses in Pompeii.

During the early Empire the propertied classes of the Mediterranean provinces generally provided the legionary tribunes and commanders of the auxiliary units, the senior tribune of the legion being appointed from the senatorial aristocracy, the highest stratum of

Roman society. These posts were held by young men at early stages in their careers, although another senior post, the fortress prefectship of a legion, was held by a former centurion subordinate only to the senior tribune. Legionary centurions were also put in charge of auxiliary units, increasingly so during the third century. We know little of the officers who commanded units during the fourth century in Britain. Presumably, as in other provinces, some were soldiers who had risen through the ranks, while others had obtained their posts by purchase or through the influence of highly placed friends or relatives.

The famous cache of Roman documents from Vindolanda illuminates aspects of a commander's life in a frontier fort during the late first and early second centuries. Among the archive of Flavius Cerialis are letters hinting at the many obligations of the commander: one asks Cerialis to recommend a man to a fellow officer, another invites Cerialis' wife to a birthday party and a third is a rather formal expression of good wishes to Cerialis in a forthcoming enterprise. Another letter from a different archive mentions the slave of an officer. The study of the houses of tribunes and commanders should show how their plans reflected the needs of the occupants for public areas where important guests could be received and entertained, for private quarters and for the accommodation of slaves and servants.

Because auxiliary commanders and legionary tribunes were of similar status, it is hardly surprising that in forts and fortresses alike their houses were of similar size and design. The model was the Mediterranean townhouse with its ranges of rooms disposed around a central courtyard. In Britain the only legionary tribunes' houses with

35 The commanding officer's house at Caernarvon with courtyard and additional range of rooms.

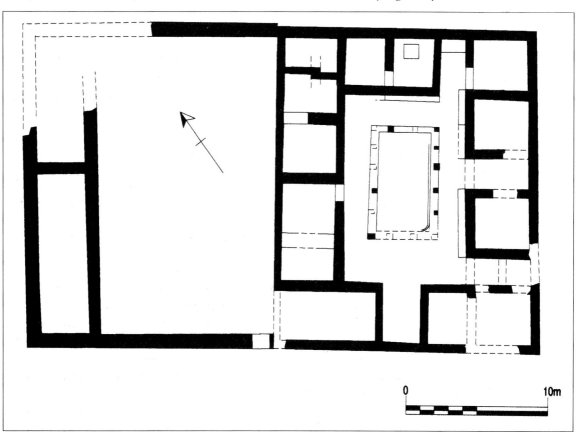

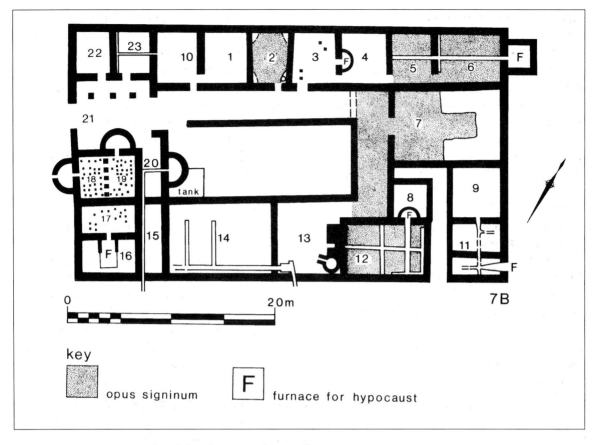

key

opus signinum   F furnace for hypocaust

36 Plan of a late Roman courtyard house at South
Shields, probably the residence of the commanding officer
(see also **70** and **colour plate 7**).

complete plans are at Inchtuthil, a fortress which
was abandoned by the middle of AD 88, before its
completion. Four houses had been built and
space had probably been allowed for three more.
The plans of three were essentially similar:
appended to the courtyard with its surrounding
ranges of rooms were a further two ranges
separated by a corridor. In the fourth house there
was a second courtyard rather than a corridor
separating the two ranges of rooms. Houses with
this type of plan also occur in forts such as
Nanstallon and Pen Llystyn, which are first
century in date, and in the later second century at
Caernarvon (**35**). At Inchtuthil the additional
ranges of rooms were interpreted as offices but
that would seem to leave very little space for the
private quarters of the tribune, his family and his
household. Inchtuthil, Nanstallon and Pen
Llystyn were all of timber construction and floor
levels, doorways and evidence of interior
decoration did not survive; this makes it difficult

even to hazard a guess at the function of most of
the rooms. Caernarvon was excavated in 1920–3
and, as is often the case with such early work, the
published report fails to describe the building in
any detail.

At South Shields the excavation of a large
courtyard house built in *c*. AD 300 has recently
been completed (**36** and **colour plate 7**).
Although it had been much damaged by
medieval stone robbers and Victorian
excavators, what remains still presents the
clearest picture from Britain of the arrangement
of an officer's house. At the centre of the
building was a rectangular courtyard containing
a water tank; on two sides of the courtyard were
wide verandahs, their roofs supported on lathe-
turned columns which sat on low walls. The

largest room (7), which measured 9m by 6.75m (29.5ft by 22ft), was entered from the verandah by a centrally placed door. Its floor was of fine brick mortar (*opus signinum*) but around the walls opposite the door was a setting of flagstones which identifies the room as a dining room (*triclinium*). When dining formally, it was the Roman custom to recline on couches set around three sides of the room; in Mediterranean houses the paving was often of marble slabs which prevented the legs of the couches from damaging the mosaic floors in the remainder of the rooms.

Room 12 was probably a second, smaller dining room heated by a hypocaust (underfloor heating system), the channels of which at one end of the room ran around the base of the walls in order to carry hot gases up through hollow tiles lining the walls. This unusual arrangement would have provided a well-heated dining area at one end of the room. It seems that in effect the house had summer and winter dining rooms (see **colour plate 6**). Room 13 was originally the kitchen with a large oven and a stoke hole for the hypocaust in the winter dining room.

Half the length of the north-west wing was occupied by a suite of four rooms (3–6) with interconnecting doors and floors of fine brick-mortar; the two end rooms were heated by a channelled hypocaust. This is the only suite in the house and can be identified as the private quarters of the commander: room 3, which had a door connecting with the verandah, was perhaps used to receive guests informally and the remaining rooms provided living and sleeping quarters. Rooms 2 and 11 had hypocausts and were perhaps for guests or other members of the household. Much of the south-west wing was occupied by a suite of baths, next to a small colonnaded entrance court where the occupant could have greeted important guests formally. Room 14 was a stable and the remaining rooms, which had earth floors, were probably service areas or store rooms.

Considerable alterations were carried out before the middle of the fourth century. These included the conversion of the north-east verandah into a lobby for the two dining rooms; the walls of the lobby were probably the source of fragments of painted plaster found nearby which depicted a cupid, the only figured wall painting known from the northern frontier.

The house was built for a senior officer, probably the commander of the garrison. It is not in the usual position on the left-hand side of the headquarters building but in the eastern corner of the fort. This is probably explained by the plan of the fort at this period which is of a distinctive late Roman type (described in Chapter 7). Another courtyard house, far larger than at South Shields, lay in the south-east corner of the fort at Piercebridge. The house at South Shields shows that throughout at least the first half of the fourth century its occupant had as much need as senior officers of the earlier empire for public rooms in which to receive and entertain guests formally. It was not until well after *c.* AD 350 that a decline in the status of the house was evident. The fine floors were covered with rough paving, the summer dining room was converted into an open yard and all the hypocausts went out of use. Only the private quarters remained intact.

Barracks in the earlier Roman period

All ranks below the legionary legate, the most senior officers of the legion and the auxiliary commander, were accommodated in barracks or, in the case of officers, in houses attached to barracks. Although there was much variation in size and detail, the essential plan of the barrack was always the same: a long narrow building was sub-divided for about two-thirds or three-quarters of its length into a series of rooms (*contubernia*) each accommodating a group of soldiers, the remainder of its length forming the house of the officer in charge of the men (**37**). Hyginus, a first- or second-century writer, describes the tented accommodation of a century in a marching camp. Eight tents 3m (10ft) square, each for eight men, were set up in a line with a larger tent for a centurion at one end (a century confusingly consisted of eighty

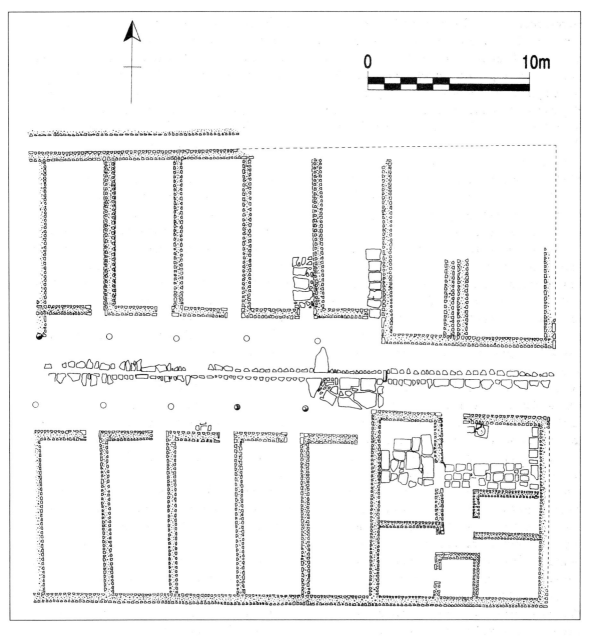

men in the period with which we are concerned and Hyginus omits tents for sixteen men assuming that that number would always be on duty). Space was allowed in front of each tent (*papilio*) for the stacking of arms and equipment (*arma*) and beyond that was an area for the tethering of the baggage train. Barrack buildings are generally supposed to have been a translation of this arrangement into permanent form (**colour plate 8**).

37 A barrack block at Chesters which was designed to accommodate two of the troops (*turmae*) of a cavalry regiment. Each *contubernium* would have been divided into two rooms by partitions; the surviving areas of paving suggest the existence of side passages. The barracks are only partly excavated and each probably included ten *contubernia*.

The officer in charge of a legionary or auxiliary century was a centurion; his cavalry equivalent was a decurion. Their accommodation varied in size according to their status. The most senior centurions were those in charge of the first cohort of a legion; at Inchtuthil they were provided with courtyard houses similar in design to those of the tribunes but smaller in area. The houses of the chief centurions at Inchtuthil and Caerleon contained hypocausts. The other legionary centurions had more modest quarters, typically consisting of a block of rooms with a central corridor running down its length, as at Gloucester, Inchtuthil, Caerleon and Chester. A recent analysis of these blocks of rooms has shown that, while their plans vary widely, they have a number of features in common, in particular a tendency for the largest and best-appointed rooms to be placed at the end of the block furthest from the main street. Little progress has been made in identifying the functions of rooms in the officers' blocks of auxiliary forts.

The internal arrangement of barracks was generally similar no matter what type of unit they housed. The *contubernia* were usually divided into two rooms, although rarely they consisted of single rooms. For how long the functions of the two rooms continued to reflect those of the tent and space for arms storage in the temporary camp is uncertain. An early modification to the plan was the introduction of a passage along the side of the front room giving access to the rear room; such passages occur in the Neronian legionary fortress at Exeter and in later barracks at South Shields, Vindolanda, Chesters and Housesteads. Hearths are often found in the front rooms of barracks, for example in the mid second-century barrack XI at Strageath and in barracks of the early third century at South Shields. Their presence suggests that the front rooms had become part of the living quarters; arms and armour were perhaps kept in arms stores (*armamentaria*) such as the building mentioned in an inscription from Lanchester.

The accommodation for the eight to ten men in a *contubernium* was far from generous. The internal floor areas generally range between 15 and 30sq m (49 and 98sq ft) and it is often suggested that tiers of bunks were provided for the men. However, the numbers actually accommodated in the barracks were probably often a fraction of the nominal strength of a unit. Reports on unit strengths from Vindolanda refer to soldiers posted away from the fort, some as far distant as London. The layout of the barracks, frequently built back to back and divided by a narrow alley, meant that the rear rooms would have received little natural light, even though finds of opaque window glass are common. There is no evidence for the existence of clerestories to provide additional light and the soldiers probably lived in crepuscular gloom, as did most people in the ancient and medieval worlds when indoors.

In many forts large ovens for communal cooking were built into the rear of the ramparts opposite the ends of the barracks. Frequent finds in barracks of querns for milling cereals by hand and sometimes, as at South Shields and Vindolanda, the survival of the actual emplacements for querns, show that the hearths in the *contubernia* were used for cooking as well as heating. At South Shields a block of six barracks built in the first half of the third century had pottery ventilators set into their roofs through which the smoke from the open hearths in the *contubernia* escaped. Other finds illustrate how the soldiers passed some of their time off duty. Stone slabs marked out as gaming boards are sometimes found and a bag containing 119 gaming counters was recovered from a barrack destroyed by fire at Ravenglass.

Barracks and the identification of units

With rare exceptions it is not until the second century that forts produce evidence, usually inscriptions, for the identity of their garrisons and only in the third century are the majority of the garrisons in Britain identifiable. Therefore the only means of recovering the disposition of units in the earlier period is the study of fort plans, particularly the number and size of barracks, in order to establish the type of unit in garrison. The table below shows the size of the various categories, their subdivisions and the number of barracks which would seem to be required for their accommodation. It should be taken with a large pinch of salt, for it represents nothing more than the best that can be done to reconcile ancient sources which are fragmentary and contradictory.

Some of the difficulties are illustrated by a late first-century strength report of *cohors I Tungrorum* from Vindolanda. Six centurions are listed, which would indicate that we are dealing with a *cohors quingenaria equitata*, a unit which consisted of six centuries according to Hyginus, a first- or second-century writer. Its paper strength would thus have been 6x80=480 men but the report gives the number of men as over 750. A diploma of AD 103 shows that by that date the unit was milliary, which means that its size had been increased to ten centuries, and the strength report has been taken to refer to a period when the unit was actually in the process of building up its numbers to milliary size. This

is a neat explanation but one which loses much of its appeal when it is realized that strength reports from elsewhere also generally show that units were grossly under or over strength.

Further difficulties arise in considering fort plans. Many forts seem to have contained more than one unit, particularly in the first century, as at Hod Hill in Dorset where the plan suggests that the garrison consisted of a legionary cohort and half of a cavalry regiment (*ala*). The converse also applies, as on the Antonine Wall where some forts were too small to house complete auxiliary units; for example the six centuries of the part-mounted *cohors IV Gallorum* probably occupied the fort at Castlehill, its four cavalry troops being accommodated at nearby Bearsden.

Two recent excavations provide more evidence for mixed garrisons in forts. At Elginhaugh perhaps the most thorough investigation of a timber fort in Britain took place in 1986 (see **18**). Excluding the buildings of the central range and a structure built against the eastern rampart there were twelve buildings in the fort. Nine barracks were identified in addition to a possible store building; there were

Table 1

The likely size of units and the number of barracks required according to their subdivisions[a]

Type of unit	Total no. of men[b]	Size of sub-unit	No. of men per barrack	No. of barracks
Cohors I of legion until c. AD 70	480	80	80	6
Cohors I of legion post AD 70	800	80	80	10
Cohors II–X	4320	80	80	54
Ala milliaria (cavalry)	768 (1000)	32	2x32	12
Ala (cavalry)	512 (500)	32	2x32	8
Cohors milliaria equitata	800+256 (1000)	80 or 32	80 or 2x32	14
Cohors milliaria	800 (1000)	80	80	10
Cohors quingenaria equitata	480+128	80 or 32	80 or 2x32	8
Cohors quingenaria	480 (500)	80	80	6

[a] These figures exclude officers and specialist workers in the legions.
[b] Nominal strength given in brackets.

also two buildings of uncertain function. The type of unit or combination of units in garrison is quite uncertain. At Strageath the Flavian fort had twelve barracks, suggesting to its excavators that the garrison consisted of two units brigaded together, and the second of the two Antonine forts at the same site again contained twelve barracks.

At Wallsend, as we have already seen in Chapter 2, matters are fairly straightforward. There was sufficient accommodation for six centuries and four troops or *turmae* of cavalry, the latter sharing two barracks. This corresponds exactly to the size of a *cohors quingenaria equitata*, a type of unit known to have been in garrison at Wallsend in the third century. In so far as their plans are known, the other forts of the Hadrian's Wall system seem to have been built for single units. In the third century, however, irregular units (*numeri*) were added to the garrisons of some forts. They were placed under the auxiliary commander but the size of these units and their internal organization are unknown.

Later Roman barracks

In the later Roman period the barrack accommodation in many auxiliary forts was radically altered. The significance of these changes is poorly understood, largely because there is so little evidence for the details of unit strength and organization in the later Roman army. Nevertheless, the study of these barracks has produced interesting ideas about the late Roman army which can be tested by new evidence from excavations.

For many decades it was believed that the garrisons in auxiliary forts gradually assumed the character of a peasant militia. Evidence for this was provided by the irregular plans of the later Roman barracks, by finds of objects with female associations and by the occasional discovery of infant burials. Abandonment of the *vici* outside forts on Hadrian's Wall until recently was supposed to have taken place some forty years before the end of Roman rule. The

inhabitants apparently moved into the forts which became, in the words of Sir Ian Richmond, 'little fortified townships, more like a medieval Conway, Beaumaris or Flint than a Roman castellum'. The result was a ramshackle settlement full of crudely constructed buildings, at the sight of which 'a centurion of the old order would have blenched'. In recent years it has been discovered that some of the *vici* on Hadrian's Wall had in fact been largely abandoned almost a century earlier than Richmond believed and that in some instances radical rebuilding of the barracks had taken place at the same time. This was taken to indicate that the downgrading of the forts and their garrisons was well under way by the end of the third century.

The type of barrack which has been associated with these changes is best seen at Housesteads where two examples (Buildings XIII and XIV) are displayed to visitors. Building XIV, which has been fully published, was built on the site of one of the original barracks of the fort but took a very different form (**38**). At the end nearest the rampart was a rectangular block with a small annexe which overlaid the officers' quarters of the earlier barrack and presumably served the same function. Then, in place of the continuous range of ten *contubernia* in the old barrack, six free-standing blocks were erected with a smaller building attached to the block at the far end. The internal arrangements of these blocks, which have been called 'chalets', appear rather haphazard with lengths of walls misaligned. There are similar plans from other forts on the northern frontier at Wallsend, Chesters, Great Chesters, Birdoswald and High Rochester, and from further afield at Malton and Caernarvon. The free-standing blocks or chalets at Malton were particularly important because their excavation in the 1920s, unfortunately poorly recorded, had produced thirty-one infant burials. Excavators at Housesteads since the beginning of this century had remarked upon the apparent abundance of articles associated

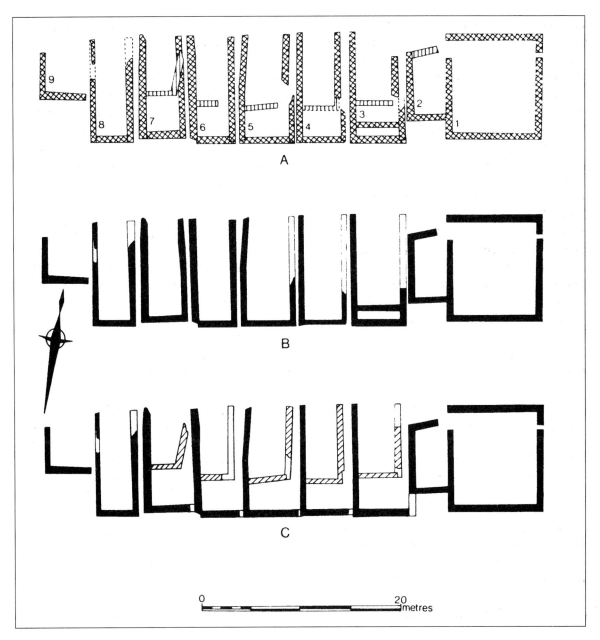

38 Later Roman barrack at Housesteads.
A: cross-hatched walls original, walls with single-line hatching are later. B: suggested original form of the barrack. C: suggested modifications to the barrack with new walls shown with single-line hatching.

with women in the late levels and it was suggested that the so-called chalets had each housed single families. The importance of this observation lay in the drastic reduction in the number of soldiers in the fort which was implied. A barrack which in the reign of Hadrian was built for eighty men was replaced in the late third century by buildings which perhaps only housed six families. Even allowing for extra buildings packed into the fort, the late

Roman unit would have been but a shadow of the earlier Roman garrison, in effect a mere 15 per cent of its original size. If, as is commonly believed, these chalets were the standard accommodation in forts on the Wall, we would have to conclude that from the end of the third century the northern frontier was held by no more than a token force.

A rather different perspective is now developing as a result of new discoveries and research. In 1980 the writer dug two barracks at Vindolanda built back to back and with side passages in their *contubernia*. At first sight they were otherwise very similar to the chalets at Housesteads. But the plans recovered when the excavation was complete showed none of the confusion of walls typical of the chalets. The barracks had been much altered but the well-preserved stratigraphy helped to establish that the modifications were not carried out at random but represented overall replannings. Moreover, their date of construction, shortly after the rebuilding of the fort in *c.* AD 223–5, was half a century earlier than the date of the Housesteads chalets. They belonged to the period when the *vici* were at their most extensive and it was difficult to believe that they were built to house soldiers and their families. In the light of the barrack plans at Vindolanda, the misalignment of various walls in Building XIV at Housesteads can be explained by showing that the barrack was first built as a series of detached blocks later amalgamated when side passages were inserted.

Recent excavations at South Shields have explored barracks of three periods on an extensive scale. The barracks of the second and third periods, dating from the early third century (39) and the late third or early fourth century, were built as continuous ranges, each containing an officer's quarters and five *contubernia*, one of the barracks of the third period (the only one of that period so far entirely excavated) having in addition a workshop adjoining the officer's quarters and two small rooms at the end of the row of *contubernia*.

The barracks at South Shields resemble those at Vindolanda and Housesteads in having only five or six *contubernia* rather than the eight to ten usually found in earlier barracks, and in the prevalence of side passages, only occasionally encountered at an earlier date. As the alterations at Housesteads demonstrate, the construction of the *contubernia* as free-standing blocks is not an essential characteristic of the type (see 38). Although High Rochester (see 7) seems to have a double barrack built back to back as at Vindolanda, the plans of chalet barracks from early excavations at other forts make little sense; no doubt walls of several periods are shown, obscuring the original plans of the barracks.

Progress in obtaining a clearer picture of the garrisons of later Roman forts has not depended entirely on new excavations. Careful study of small finds – objects of personal adornment such as earrings, finger rings and hair pins as well as implements, shoes and so on – have shown that items with female associations are no more common in the later levels of Roman forts on the northern frontier than in earlier levels, contrary to what was claimed by the excavators of Housesteads.

The problem of infant burials in forts is more difficult. With the exception of South Shields, they are known only from excavations carried out many years ago and only at Malton and South Shields have they been recovered from a barrack. One of the infant burials from South Shields was found in what was probably the under-officer's quarters of a barrack built in the first decade of the third century and occupied for perhaps less than twenty years. Two other infant burials in barracks were dated to the mid-fourth century and to the fourth century or later. Such burials are encountered much more commonly on civilian sites and a recent study of a large sample has shown that the majority are the result of infanticide rather than natural death at, or shortly after, birth. Some infants were buried under the floors of living quarters, perhaps in the belief that their spirits in some

1 The *caldarium* (hot, damp room) of the baths in the fortress of the Second Augustan Legion at Exeter. The view is across the width of the room looking towards semi-circular and rectangular recesses. The floor of the hypocaust basement is of brick and is covered by a grid of brick supports for the heated floor of the room above. The walls above the hypocaust belong to the later civilian basilica which incorporated much of the fabric of the baths.

2 Hadrian's Wall running eastwards from Housesteads; view from the interior of the fort.

3 Conjectural reconstruction of the legionary compounds
at Corbridge. They appear to date from the early third
century and occupied the centre of a Roman town that
serviced the needs of the soldiers on Hadrian's Wall.

The most northerly Gateway in the East rampart of Birdoswald — outside view

4 Watercolour by D. Mossman of the west gate at Birdoswald in 1857, an accurate representation which was published as an engraving. By the mid-nineteenth century there were many similar records of the better-preserved masonry of forts on Hadrian's Wall and the Saxon Shore.

5 The reconstructed west gate at South Shields, completed in 1988. This was built on the original foundations of the Roman gate, which were protected by a concrete cap. Based on detailed research, the appearance of the gate has been accepted as a reasonable interpretation of the available evidence, both from the site itself and by analogy with better-preserved gates.

6 Wall and projecting towers of the Saxon Shore fort at Pevensey. These well-preserved defences were built on a much larger scale than those of stone forts of the second and earlier third centuries.

7 Conjectural reconstruction of the late Roman courtyard house at South Shields. See **36** and text for the function of the rooms.

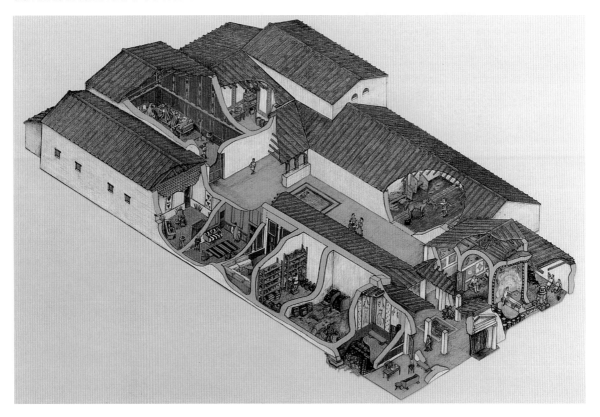

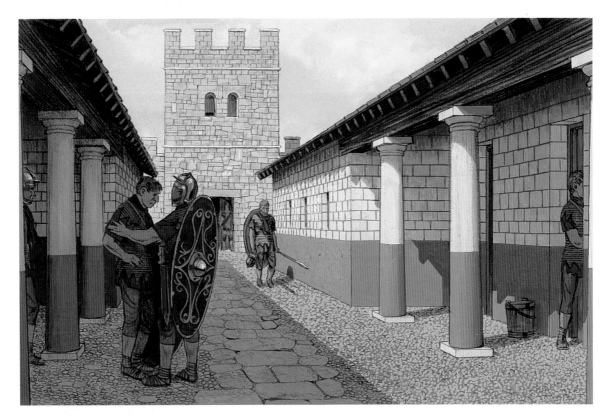

8 Conjectural reconstruction of barracks at Chesters. It was normal practice to paint the exteriors of Roman buildings in bright colours (to modern eyes more suited to the Mediterranean than the variable climate of northern Britain). The verandas allowed the best use of daylight while giving some shelter from the elements.

9 Conjectural reconstruction of the interior of the headquarters cross hall of the legionary fortress at York, following rebuilding in the early fourth century. The scene is dominated by a statue of Constantine; a head of Constantine, twice life-size, was found before 1823 in or near the headquarters building. Other statues include earlier emperors, to the right against the columns. To the right are iron railings, probably enclosing altars (the headquarters of forts of this period were similarly congested with statues and altars). To the rear is a tribunal. The columns of the nave might have supported flat lintels rather than arches, although the latter are more typical of late Roman architecture. One of the columns can be seen re-erected outside York Minster and the remains of the headquarters building are strikingly displayed beneath the Minster.

10 Head pot from Piercebridge. A female head is represented with an elaborate hairstyle which is very carefully depicted. This may be a portrait of Julia Domna, wife of Emperor Septimius Severus. The vessel was probably made at York, where a number of similar head pots are known; their manufacture seems to have been introduced by North Africans serving in the Roman army in Britain.

11 A member of the re-enactment group Quinta in reconstructed scale armour, as worn by the *catafractarii* or heavy cavalry of the later Roman army.

12 Painting which reconstructs the contents of a wooden chest excavated at Corbridge in 1964. It was buried in the Hadrianic period near the headquarters building of the fort which preceded the town at Corbridge. The most important objects are the iron strip armour but there are dozens of other objects, most of them typical finds on military sites. None is of particular value and the contents of the chest seem to be merely a collection of scrap metal.

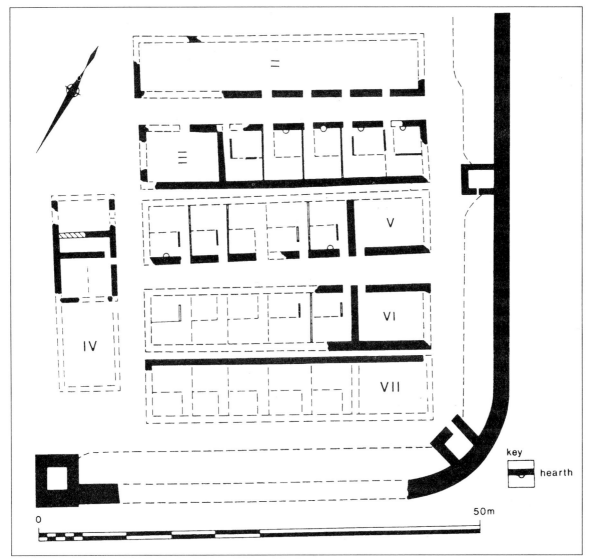

39 Barracks of the second period of the supply base at South Shields, built in *c.* AD 222–35. Each barrack has five *contubernia* and an officer's house.

way could maintain a link with their parents, and others were buried in special cemeteries next to houses. However, some were associated with the construction of houses or of installations such as corn-drying ovens, as if they could offer protection to the structures and those who used them. It is therefore not always clear what isolated infant burials mean. In forts they do not necessarily indicate the presence of families living in barracks. An exception occurs at Malton where the recovery of up to thirty-one burials from what seems to have been a single barrack can perhaps only be explained by the presence of families, but at what date and in

what circumstances are matters for speculation.

Perhaps the reduction in the number of *contubernia* in these barracks is their most significant aspect. The presence of only five or six *contubernia* rather than the eight to ten usually found in earlier barracks might simply mean that the strength of the centuries was reduced by about 40 per cent, that is from 80 to 48 men. The dates of the Vindolanda and South Shields barracks indicate that this took place in

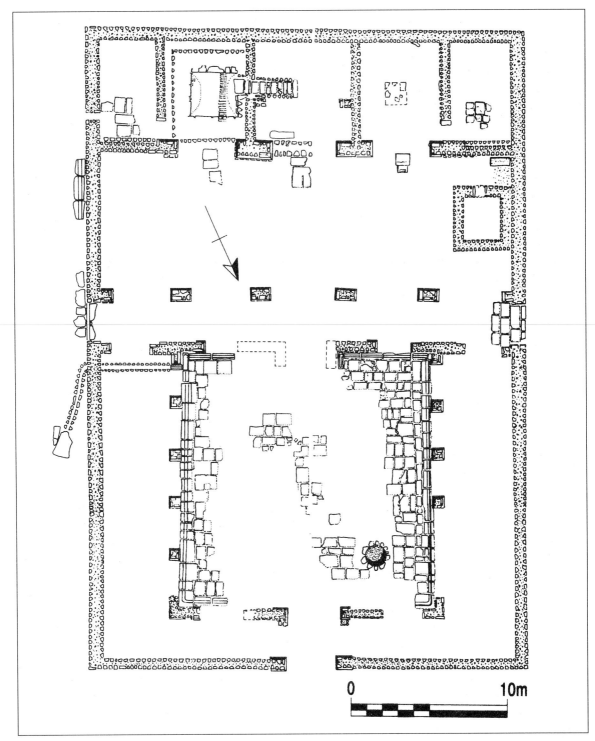

40 The headquarters building at Chesters, as now displayed. When the strongroom (in the south range of rooms, east of the central room) was discovered in 1803, its original wooden door sheathed in iron plates still survived. The remainder of the building was excavated between 1870 and 1875. Its large size reflects the high status of the *ala* which garrisoned the fort.

the first half of the third century. The overall reduction in the size of the garrisons was perhaps not as drastic, for it is during this period that irregular units were installed in some forts alongside the regular auxiliary units. Buildings inserted along the backs of the fort walls may have been for their accommodation.

The headquarters building (principia)

At the centre of every fort stood the headquarters building, the Latin name for which was *principia* (a plural noun), originally denoting an open space in a camp where the standards of the army were kept and which was bordered by the tents of the commander and his staff. In first- and second-century forts the *principia* consisted of three elements: a cross-hall, so named because it lay across the main axis of the whole building, a shrine for the standards of the unit which opened off the rear of the cross-hall and which was flanked on either side by two rooms to accommodate pay and record clerks, and, on the other side of the cross-hall, a forecourt which was usually surrounded by verandahs (40). This complex stood at the junction of the two main streets, the *viae praetoria* and *principalis*, where its main entrance was situated.

Many early excavations in forts concentrated on the central range of buildings, and particularly on the headquarters building. The result is that, although we have dozens of plans of headquarters buildings, detailed knowledge of their history and the activities carried out in them is based largely on a handful of examples excavated in more recent times. Most informative has been the work carried out on the headquarters buildings of the legionary fortresses at Caerleon and York (**colour plate 9**), where much has been learnt about the arrangements in the cross-hall. Examples in auxiliary forts such as Carrawburgh, South Shields and Wallsend, which have been excavated using modern techniques, have been less well preserved but have yielded valuable information.

The headquarters building was the nerve centre of a fort or fortress, providing accommodation for its administration and a setting for the enforcement of discipline and the observances of military religion. The importance of these functions is illustrated by the provision of temporary accommodation for them while a fort or fortress was being built. In the unfinished fortress at Inchtuthil a small timber headquarters building occupied part of the plot reserved for a full-size headquarters building. Its site probably coincided exactly with that of the intended forecourt of the larger building; the smaller building would have remained in use until its functions could be transferred to its permanent replacement. In the fort at South Shields built in the mid-Antonine period, a shrine for the standards and two flanking offices, part of the rear range of the intended headquarters building, were among the first structures to be built. Work on the remainder was postponed until a later stage, by which time the overall plan had been altered, so that the shrine and flanking offices had to be rebuilt. A probable example of a free-standing shrine which actually survived to be incorporated in a completed headquarters building occurs at Brecon Gaer.

The shrine of the standards was the focus of the headquarters building, lying on its central axis and opening off the cross-hall, from which in stone-built forts it was divided by low screen-slabs surmounted by iron grilles (**41**). Excavation has recovered very little evidence for the interior arrangements of these shrines. In timber forts floor levels seldom survive; in stone forts the shrine was often built above a subterranean strongroom, the collapse or robbing of which will have destroyed the floor of the shrine. At Vindolanda, instead of a strongroom, there were stone-lined pits arranged to form three sides of an open square; these would have held massive wooden or iron chests (**42**). The arrangement of the pits suggests that there was a large feature in the centre of the room. This would not have been a statue of the

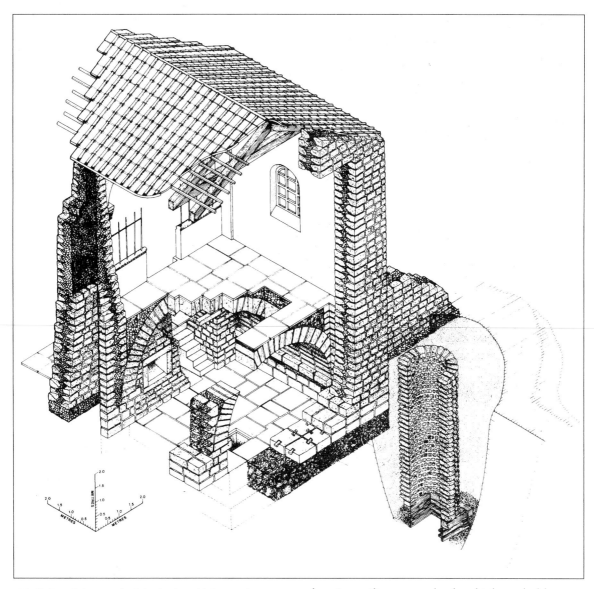

41 Shrine of the standards in the late third- or early fourth-century headquarters building at South Shields. The shrine is raised above the floor of the cross-hall to the left, on a platform formed by the vaulted roof of the strongroom beneath, and is entered by steps down from the cross-hall. The well was dug in an earlier period, when the forecourt lay on the site of the rear range which includes the shrine of the standards.

emperor, as is sometimes supposed, but a base which supported the standards of the unit (**43**). From Corbridge and from Vindolanda itself there are fragments of carved stone friezes showing military standards which probably decorated the sides of the bases.

Imperial and religious dedications were made in the cross-hall and in the forecourt. In the cross-hall at Caerleon a screen of columns stood before the entrance to the shrine of standards. In front of the columns bases of various sizes were found; they had supported bronze statues greater than life size, small fragments of which were found nearby. Immediately opposite, on the other side of the cross-hall, was a large area enclosed by iron railings which was thought to have been a sacred area reserved for one or

42 Masonry-lined pits in the shrine of the standards in the headquarters building at Vindolanda. They would have held wooden or iron chests where the funds of the garrison were stored.

more large altars. There were also statue bases and a railed-off enclosure in the cross-hall at York in the *principia* which was rebuilt in the late third or early fourth century (see **colour plate 9**). Finds of statue bases, large altars and fragments of bronze statuary are known from a number of forts. Statue bases remain in position in the cross-halls at Housesteads and at Brough-by-Bainbridge. At Caernarvon and in the late third- or early fourth-century headquarters building at South Shields, there were strips of paving running across the width of the cross-hall at its centre; these may have been provided as a solid base for statues or altars, concentrated, as at Caerleon, in the area in front of the shrine of the standards. The cross-hall of a fort was not much smaller than the nave of a medieval English church; by the late third century a cross-hall was probably as cluttered with accumulations of statues and altars as a church was with tombs and statues of saints on the eve of the Reformation.

43 Relief of Hercules from the headquarters building in the west compound at Corbridge; it depicts one of the Labours of Hercules, the slaying of the Lernean hydra, and probably adorned the masonry base which supported the legionary standards.

44 Mid-nineteenth-century engraving of the strongroom at High Rochester. The steps led down from the cross-hall of the headquarters building. The door consisted of a single slab of stone on wheels and running in a groove; the arch to the right is the mouth of a drain.

In early forts the funds of the unit and the savings of the soldiers were probably placed in the shrine; its sacred nature should have made it inviolable and to make doubly sure a permanent guard was posted outside. In later stone-built headquarters buildings subterranean strongrooms were often inserted beneath the shrine or an adjacent room (**44**). A comparison of strongroom sizes shows that in some circumstances they served special purposes: the strongroom built at South Shields when the fort was converted into a supply base in the Severan period is three times larger than the average, presumably because it held bullion and other valuables in transit. At Maryport, perhaps also a supply base, there is again a strongroom of exceptionally large size.

The forecourt and cross-hall of a headquarters building were areas where large numbers of people could assemble. The cross-hall, although by no means large enough to hold an entire garrison, provided space for activities such as courts martial, the formal issuing of orders and passwords, and religious observances. The commanding officer presided over these events from a raised platform or tribunal which was always placed at the left-hand end of the hall (from the point of view of someone looking towards the front of the fort); in the second century the strongroom was sometimes placed below the tribunal. His house was usually sited to the right of the headquarters building; at South Shields, Wallsend and Newcastle, small doors were placed at the right-hand end of the cross-hall and in the side of the house, facing each other across the street separating the two buildings. In the headquarters building at York there was a special entrance for the legate through the rear range which was opposite his palace. These arrangements would have allowed the commanding officer to make a formal entrance directly from his house into the cross-hall, proceeding down its length through the ranks of his men to gain his seat on the tribunal. Such analyses of building plans provide occasional glimpses of the military ceremonial which would have governed the use of many parts of the fort. In any closed hierarchical society specific routes and spaces acquire special significance.

In most forecourts there are wells or sometimes tanks. These have sometimes been seen as emergency reserves of water, provided so that there was a supply within the fort in case it came under attack. Some of these wells are quite deep but many are shallow and must have had only a small capacity. It seems more likely that their purpose was to provide water for religious ceremonies in the headquarters building. This seems to be confirmed by the sequence of construction in the mid-Antonine fort at South Shields, where a well was dug at the same time as the free-standing shrine of the standards and offices were built, in advance of the construction of the remainder of the building.

The plans of headquarters buildings show little development during the Roman period in Britain. At Newcastle, Corbridge (east compound) and South Shields, the forecourt was omitted from headquarters buildings dating to the later second century and early third century. This was perhaps because of lack of space rather than because of any change in military ceremonial; headquarters buildings with conventional plans continued to be built in the earlier third century, as at Vindolanda, and down to the end of the third century or early fourth century, as in the case of a later example at South Shields. However, the headquarters building in the west compound at Corbridge is an early example of the basilica plan: the axis of the hall ran down its length rather than across its width, as was the case with cross-halls, and the rear range was replaced by rooms on either side of the hall with the shrine placed at the end opposite the entrance. This was a plan typical of late Roman forts in the east but became prevalent at too late a date to be found elsewhere in Britain.

Other buildings

For all the occupants of a fort, apart from the commander, living conditions were cramped. This shortage of space was sometimes partly alleviated by the construction of verandahs along the front of barracks. In some forts in other provinces additional space was also provided by porticos along the main streets; these were included in the reconstruction of South Shields in the late third or early fourth century and may have existed in the mid-second-century fort. In legionary fortresses centurions were provided with meeting halls (*scholae*). A large hypocausted room added to the rear of the headquarters building at Caernarvon might have served this purpose; there is a hypocausted room in a similar position in the fort at Newcastle.

Large halls were added to the front of the headquarters buildings at Brecon Gaer, Ribchester, Halton Chesters, Newstead and Wallsend. It is uncertain whether these are drill halls of the type mentioned in an inscription from Netherby and described by Vegetius, a late Roman writer on military matters. There is an aisled hall in the northern part of the fort at Birdoswald which might have served as a drill hall.

Courtyard buildings in or behind the central range have long been identified as hospitals (*valetudinaria*); conclusive evidence of their function has never been forthcoming from auxiliary forts, but much larger courtyard buildings in fortresses have been satisfactorily identified as hospitals. The case for their presence in forts has been strengthened by a document from Vindolanda which mentions soldiers at, or possibly building, a *valetudinarium*. Granaries and workshops are described in Chapter 6.

5
Outside the fort

Settlements outside forts

All forts occupied for any considerable length of time developed extramural settlements known as *vici*, and outside well-established fortresses there were very large settlements which could attain the status of a city. It has to be acknowledged that the study of these settlements has always been eclipsed by the excavation of forts and fortresses. This imbalance is so great that it has even led to extravagant suggestions that further examination of forts should be embargoed until the problems of the *vici* have been tackled. No underestimate of the importance of these problems is intended, even though this discussion confines itself mainly to those aspects which shed light on the function of forts.

Only two *vici* in Britain, those at Vindolanda (45) and Housesteads, have been examined on a large scale, but the plans of others are known through aerial photography. By far the commonest type of building which occurs is the strip house, a rectangular building with its short side facing onto the street. Their size varies considerably, but many are large with floor areas in excess of 50sq m (538sq ft). Among those which have been excavated, there are some which served partly as shops: at Housesteads one example has a stone sill with slots and sockets for removable shutters, so that the whole street frontage could be opened up during the day to admit light and display wares for sale; in a strip house at Vindolanda, just inside the door opening onto the street, there is an L-shaped foundation for a counter, of the same type as complete counters which can still be seen at Pompeii and Ostia. Such details are sufficient to confirm that the strip houses in *vici* belong to an urban type of building that was widespread in the Roman world (and with close analogies in medieval towns). The front of the house served as a shop, often combining the sale and manufacture of goods, while the rear part served as the living quarters of the owner and his or her dependants. There may have been an upper storey, providing extra accommodation or storage space.

The fort baths (described in the next section) were usually sited in the *vici*. Large courtyard buildings consisting of ranges of small rooms are known at Newstead, Brecon Gaer, Chesters and Vindolanda; at Vindolanda the building incorporates a baths-suite, and at Newstead there is an adjacent, free-standing block of baths. These buildings are usually described as *mansiones*, that is inns for official travellers where overnight lodging befitting their status and perhaps a change of horses were provided. At Corbridge, Carlisle, Benwell and elsewhere, there are buildings which have also been claimed as *mansiones*, chiefly on the grounds that they have more complex plans than strip houses: they might simply represent the houses of wealthier inhabitants.

More extensive excavations might add other more specialized building types, such as warehouses, brothels, market halls and civic meeting houses, to the meagre list above. This is unlikely to alter to any degree our present perception of *vici* as mostly consisting of strip houses occupied by people engaged in trade and manufacture. Abundant evidence of industry has been recovered, including the working of iron, copper alloy, silver and gold, and of wood, bone and leather. A pottery shop has been found at Castleford, and the range of artefacts recovered by excavation, including metalwork, jewellery and coins, indicates that the standard of living was no lower in the *vici* than in the forts.

In some respects the economic basis of the *vici* seems to have been similar to that of the small towns in the civilian parts of Britain: they were centres for small-scale industry and trade in goods on a modest scale. The most telling difference is the compactness of most *vici* plans: although the areas occupied by many small towns are larger than those of *vici*, many of the buildings are spaced relatively far apart. The planning of *vici* often denied the inhabitants gardens or yards next to their houses, as in *vicus* II at Vindolanda. The houses in small towns were often built on plots and sometimes produce evidence for the processing of cereals in the form of corn-drying ovens and malting floors. Installations of this type are not yet known in *vici*, although at Wallsend,

Housesteads, Croy Hill and Carriden there are small fields or allotments on the fringes of the settlements. There were water-mills near the forts at Greatchesters and Chesters, but the insertion of the leat supplying the mill at Chesters through the base of the east tower guarding the majestic road bridge, and also through the approach ramp, suggests that the mill was built by the garrison rather than by a civilian from the *vicus*.

So much for the character of these extramural settlements. What can they tell us about the function of forts? First, they account for the absence in forts of large storehouses for consumable items (assuming that granaries were principally intended for the storage of cereals, especially wheat). Forts depended on their *vici* for the supply of goods and other services which made life for the soldiers bearable, even enjoyable, rather than merely possible. Questions of morale were involved, and some degree of official intervention in the establishment and administration of *vici* is probable, though unproven. The regularity of the *vici* plans at Vindolanda, Greta Bridge and Old Carlisle suggest that the plots were laid out

45 The two periods of the *vicus* at Vindolanda. The first *vicus* dates from the Hadrianic period; the second *vicus* was built in the early third century and given up by *c.* AD 270.

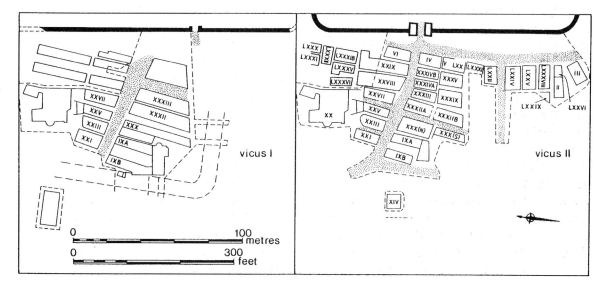

46 Aerial photograph of the fort and *vicus* of Vindolanda. The visible remains belong to the third-century fort and its civilian settlement, the latter in the foreground. Below the skyline is Barcombe Hill, source of much of the stone used in building the fort.

by the army. Once houses were built and occupied, the community probably acted autonomously as far as its own affairs were concerned. Inscriptions record dedications made by the inhabitants of the *vicus* acting in concert at Vindolanda, Carriden and Old Carlisle, and a record of a decree from Housesteads suggests that the decisions of the community had legal force. The most decisive military intervention was probably the inducement offered to traders and craftsmen to settle in the *vici* through the rewards of business in supplying the garrisons.

No *vicus* has been excavated extensively enough to determine how many houses it contained. The most reliable estimate can be made at Vindolanda, where natural topography and the evidence of aerial photographs indicate the limits of the settlement (**46**). About thirty houses belonging to the third-century *vicus* (*vicus* II) have been excavated, and there seems to be space for about the same number again. *Vici* elsewhere were much larger, as at Chesters and Old Carlisle; at the latter site buildings extend for at least 0.5km (600 yards) along the main road near the fort, and minor roads leading off it are also lined with buildings. Differences in the size and prosperity of the *vici* could have had as much to do with their geographical position as with the size and status of the forts with which they were associated.

Some, by virtue of their siting at important road junctions, might have flourished as centres for the redistribution of goods to other *vici*, while others, less successful, depended entirely on their adjacent forts for their livelihood.

Some *vici* were provided with defences, indicating that their localities had become unsettled and that open settlements were thought liable to attack. Many first-century forts had defended annexes which were also a feature of forts on the Antonine Wall. The size of these annexes varies considerably and their function is far from clear. The smaller examples were perhaps nothing more than wagon parks. The annexes of the Antonine Wall forts, usually at least half as large as their attached forts (and at Cadder and Rough Castle actually larger than their forts), sometimes contained the fort baths

as well as timber buildings of uncertain character. It is by no means certain that these larger annexes were defended *vici*. An undoubted example occurs at Malton in the late second or early third century: a wall and bank ran from the eastern corner of the fort down to the riverside, and another wall, yet to be discovered, would have enclosed an area of 3.25ha (8 acres) which contained typical *vicus* buildings (47). An inscription of AD 205–7 from Bainbridge records the building of 'a branch-

47 The *vicus* at Malton, defended by two walls (the western not yet traced by excavation) running from the corners of the fort to the River Derwent. The settlement was occupied into the second half of the fourth century, in contrast to other *vici*. Immediately south of the river at Norton there was also a large area of occupation.

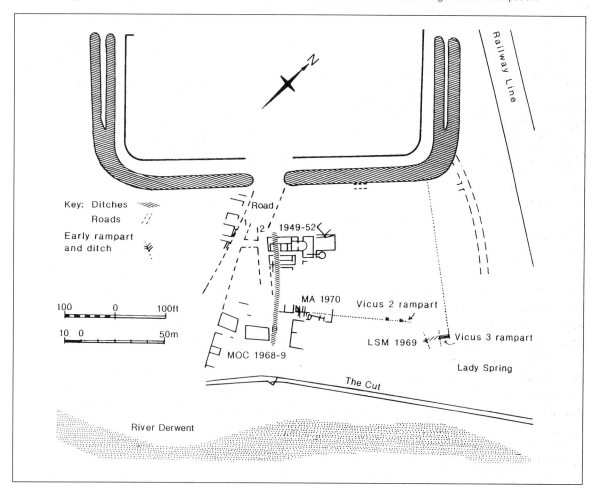

wall of roughly-hewn stone' which might have been a wall defending a *vicus*. Some 50m (55 yards) west of the fort at Wallsend a bank and ditch dating to the same general period as the defences at Malton ran from the rear of Hadrian's Wall towards the River Tyne; it perhaps enclosed the *vicus* which occupied the area between the fort and the riverside, the defences of the east side being provided by the final, eastern length of Hadrian's Wall which extended from the south-eastern corner of the fort at least as far as the low-water mark of the Tyne which is tidal at this point (see **cover illustration**).

For knowledge about the population of the *vici*, we depend largely on inscribed tombstones; these suggest that foreigners were well represented. There are Palmyrenes at South Shields (**48**) and Corbridge, a Syrian at Auchendavy, Germans at Chesters and Carrawburgh, and women from Raetia (parts of southern Germany including Bavaria) at Netherby, from Dalmatia at Carvoran and probably from Spain at Birrens. Northern forts have also produced tombstones dedicated to provincials from southern Britain. There is not much evidence of retired soldiers, but the total number of relevant inscriptions is too small to argue that the under-representation of any group is necessarily significant.

The history of the *vici* reflects their function and shows how the livelihoods of their populations depended on the garrisons of the forts. Because of lack of excavation, little can be said of their earlier history. However, the abandonment of *vicus* I at Vindolanda in the late second century, when there was also an apparent reduction in numbers of the garrison, might be explained by the complete dependence of the *vicus* dwellers on the economic needs of the fort. Much more can be said about the date at which *vici* were finally abandoned. Until recently it was assumed that *vici* continued in occupation until the Picts' War in AD 367; in the aftermath, at forts on Hadrian's Wall and further to the south, it seemed safer to house

civilians within the defences. We now know that many *vici* were apparently abandoned, or were at least much reduced in size, a century earlier. Large coin series from Vindolanda make it certain that the entire excavated area of the *vicus* was abandoned by the AD 270s; the extensive *vicus* excavations at Housesteads also produced very little fourth-century material. There are a number of *vici* elsewhere that conform to this pattern, although excavations have been on a smaller scale: Watercrook, Manchester, Ribchester, Old Penrith and Wallsend. Greta Bridge survived to the end of the third century or the early fourth century, but Malton has the only *vicus* certainly known to

48 Tombstone from South Shields dedicated to the memory of Regina, a Catuvellaunian woman (from a tribal area centred around Verulamium, modern St Albans) who was the wife and former slave of Barates, a Palmyrene. The tombstone was carved by a sculptor trained at Palmyra, a great desert city in Syria, and appended to the main Latin text is a sorrowing epitaph in Aramaic, the language of Palmyra.

have flourished throughout much of the fourth century along with a number of villas in the Vale of Pickering (**49**). Within the shelter of its walls its inhabitants prospered to the extent that one house had a mosaic floor, the only example known from a *vicus* in Britain.

All the forts with which the *vici* listed above were associated are known to have remained in occupation throughout much if not all of the fourth century; Watercrook, Old Penrith and Greta Bridge, although largely unexcavated, have certainly produced some fourth-century finds. The most likely reasons for the abandonment of these *vici* concern changes in the Roman army. In the third century payments to soldiers began to be made partly in kind, with food and other goods taking the place of cash payments. The mechanisms by which these commodities were obtained and distributed are obscure, but the resulting decrease in the amount of coinage used by soldiers is certainly evident in the fourth century when coin lists from forts are compared with those from civilian sites. This decrease in cash available for spending was accompanied by a reduction in the size of units. If the evidence of the barracks at South Shields, Vindolanda and elsewhere is to be relied upon (Chapter 4), this process began in the first half of the third century; for a time, at least at some forts, the presence of irregular units probably disguised these reductions, but unit sizes continued to decline. If *vici* depended more or less entirely on their adjacent forts, the decline in the number of soldiers and their spending power might have fatally damaged the economic basis of many of these settlements. The survival of the *vicus* at Malton might be accounted for by its wider contacts: it had a flourishing pottery industry which sent its products to the northern frontier. Other *vici* at coastal forts with ports perhaps also continued to flourish. The two towns on the northern frontier, at Corbridge and Carlisle, survived throughout the fourth century. Together with a few surviving *vici*, they could have provided a network of market and supply centres sufficient

49 Approximate limits of the villa and military zones of Britain in the later second to fourth centuries. There is a significant overlapping of the zones in south Wales and north-east England.

to meet the needs of the forts where the *vici* had been abandoned before the end of the third century.

The fort baths

In great cities and small towns, in villas and at forts, the men and women of the Roman world spent much of their leisure time at the baths. In Rome the baths built by the emperors could be used by thousands at one time; in private houses bath-suites were only large enough for the owners and their guests and servants. No matter what the scale of these buildings, their design depended on the same method of bathing (**50**). After undressing, bathers entered an unheated room and plunged into a bath of cold water; next to it was a room heated to a moderate temperature, or, in more elaborate baths, two or more rooms, some containing baths of tepid water. The last room in the series was heated to a high temperature and had as humid an atmosphere as possible, produced by steam from hot baths and from water evaporating on the heated floor surface. In baths of modest size the bathers then retraced

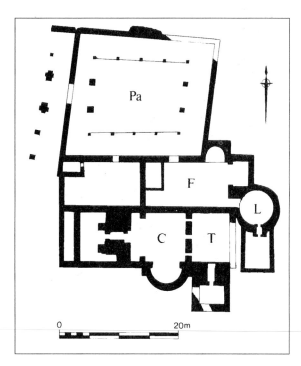

50 Plan of the baths at Red House, Corbridge, erected in the Flavian period. They were probably built for the use of soldiers in the adjacent vexillation fortress. On the north side is an exercise courtyard or *palaestra*, a feature usually lacking in baths built for auxiliaries; the baths block consists of a cold room or *frigidarium* (F), hot, dry room or *laconicum* (L), warm room or *tepidarium* (T) and hot, damp room or *caldarium* (C). The remaining rooms are for servicing the baths.

the legionary fortress of Vindonissa in Switzerland and were constructed of wood and clay, with floors and baths lined with lead sheeting. No other wooden baths are known, stone construction being otherwise universal because of the constant risk of fire. It is possible that in the Tiberian period some sort of standing order or strictly observed convention forbidding the construction of masonry buildings in forts and fortresses was in operation, and that these timber baths were devised to meet the letter, if not the spirit, of such a prohibition. The official attitude obviously changed in the reign of Claudius when magnificent stone baths were built in the fortress, replacing the timber baths. From then on, baths were a standard feature of fortresses, as at Exeter and Usk in the Neronian period and at Caerleon in the Flavian period. There are no suggestions of military austerity in the decoration of fortress baths. Exeter, Caerleon and Chester had mosaic pavements and, at the first two of these, Purbeck marble and other decorative building stones were used in profusion, although there was no imported marble.

These are the only buildings within forts and fortresses in Britain with mosaics. The absence of this ostentatious luxury from the houses of senior officers and from headquarters buildings can only be accounted for by standing orders and conventions, the existence of which has already been inferred to explain the construction of wooden baths at Vindonissa. There are no clear references in the literary sources to such regulations, although in the *Augustan Histories* Hadrian's order to demolish dining rooms, porticos, covered galleries and ornamental gardens in forts may represent an attempt to enforce military austerity.

The provision of baths in forts and fortresses was thus probably not at the discretion of individual commanders but was rather a matter of overall army discipline. In Britain baths are not found at auxiliary forts until the later first century, when they occur at Elginhaugh, abandoned in *c.* AD 86, and at Vindolanda

their route; in larger baths there were separate series of rooms for the return to the cold room which replicated those through which bathers had approached the hot room. All but the smallest baths also had a very hot dry room which opened off the cold room or the adjacent moderately heated room; this offered a quicker method of bathing, with more immediate extremes of temperature.

The gradual introduction of baths into military life during the first century tells us a great deal about the attitude of the authorities towards the army. No baths have been recognized at Augustan military sites in Germany. The earliest military baths, dating to *c.* AD 25–30, are most unusual. They occur at

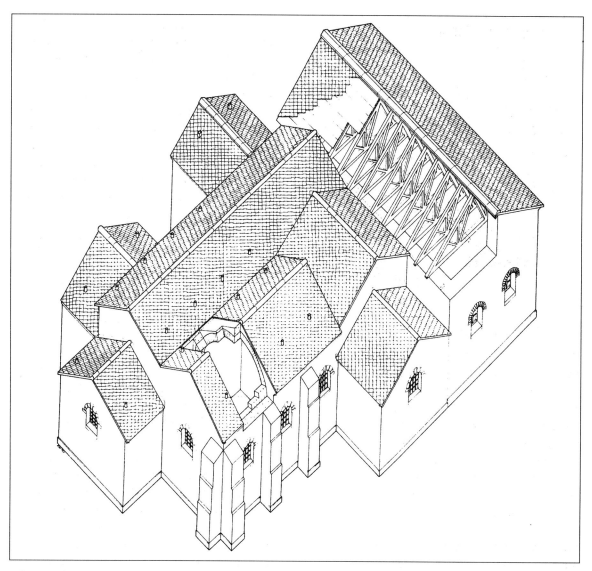

51 Conjectural reconstruction of the baths at Bewcastle. They are of a standard Hadrianic plan found at a number of forts on or near Hadrian's Wall.

where a document, dated to 25th April of a year between *c*. AD 95 and 105, tells us that eighteen soldiers were working on the baths (which have yet to be found). At about this time baths were also beginning to appear at forts in the frontier areas of mainland Europe.

The decision to provide bathing facilities for auxiliaries acknowledged changes in their cultural backgrounds. In the earlier first century they had been recruited or pressed into service from newly conquered peoples. As Roman styles of living came to be established in new provinces, later generations of recruits would have regarded baths as an essential part of daily routine. By the time that baths were provided for auxiliaries the plans of auxiliary forts were well established by convention or prescript. The result was that there was no space that could be allotted to baths, and they were built outside forts. There are a few exceptions to this rule: one is Bewcastle, an outpost fort beyond Hadrian's Wall, where for greater security the baths were contained within the irregular circuit of the defences (**51**). Exceptions also occur on

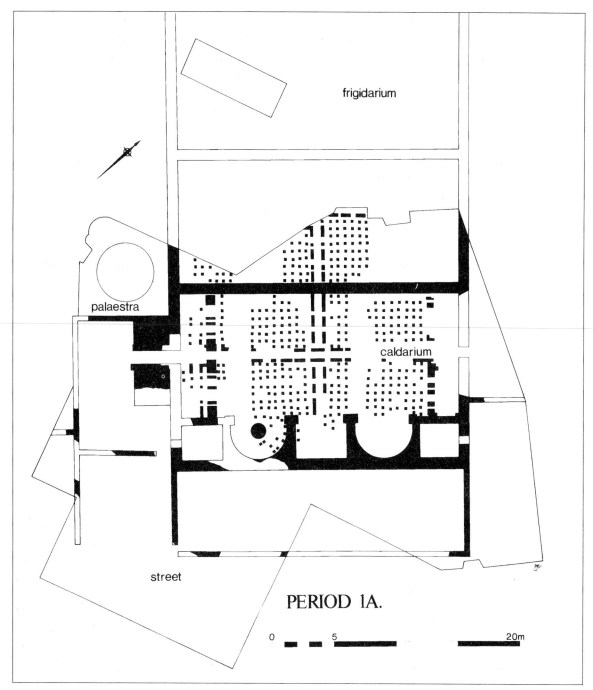

frigidarium

palaestra

caldarium

street

PERIOD 1A.

0 — 5 20m

52 The Neronian legionary baths at Exeter. The small squares in the *caldarium* and adjacent *tepidarium* are brick supports for the floor of the room; in the space created by these supports hot air circulated from furnaces at the ends of the rooms, and then passed up cavities in the walls.

the Antonine Wall, where baths were built within the defended annexes of forts, or inside forts, where they were fitted awkwardly into spaces behind the ramparts.

The legionary baths at Exeter (**52**) and Caerleon, together with those at Vindonissa in Switzerland, are of great architectural interest.

Their plans are symmetrical about their long axes, a feature lacking in early Roman baths in Italy and elsewhere. This symmetry also distinguishes the complex plans of baths of the imperial type, and it is likely that these legionary baths represent an early stage in their development. In general the baths built in the towns of Britain and other north-western provinces merely continue the loose planning of the early Roman type. The buildings supplied for the use of the legionaries were thus in the mainstream of contemporary architectural development and were presumably designed by architects who had worked on large imperial buildings. Their services were perhaps secured by legionary legates, acting in much the same way as city magistrates who marked their terms of office by erecting large public buildings.

Auxiliary baths usually had simple plans but at six forts in northern Britain – Benwell, Carrawburgh, Chesters, Bewcastle, Netherby and Ravenglass (the last being the most completely preserved building in Roman Britain,

53) – there are baths which display more sophisticated arrangements. Their almost identical plans are a skilful compression of the 'ring-type' of baths: the bather, having passed from the cold room through the tepid room to the hot room, instead of returning the same way, went into another tepid room to reach the cold room again. These baths represent a type, with no close parallels elsewhere, which was devised specially for the enormous programme of fort-building which accompanied the construction of Hadrian's Wall.

Bathing remained a part of military life throughout the Roman occupation of Britain (54). In the middle of the fourth century baths were built at Binchester; apart from the Yorkshire signal stations they represent the

53 The baths outside the fort at Ravenglass, the most completely preserved building in Roman Britain. View through door into cold room, showing niche in rear wall perhaps for a statue of Fortuna, a common dedication in baths.

54 Remains of the baths at Lancaster. They remained in use until the early fourth century when they were destroyed by the construction of a coastal fort comparable to those on the Saxon Shore. The ditch of the fort can be seen cutting through a heated room, beyond which can be seen remains of a projecting tower of the fort (part of the Wery Wall).

latest securely dated building of any architectural pretension known from any fort in Britain.

At Caerleon finds from the drain of the cold room tell us much about the use of the baths. Hair-pins, beads and other items of jewellery occurred in sufficient quantity to suggest that women used the baths regularly; the recovery of milk teeth indicates the presence of children. They would have been members of the families of officers and soldiers, the women customarily bathing in the morning before the baths attained their full temperature. A lead admission token, also from the drain, confirms that use of the baths was a privilege granted to civilians, perhaps including traders and craftsmen from the town outside the fortress.

Cemeteries

A potentially rich source of information about soldiers and the inhabitants of *vici* are the cemeteries which lay beyond the fringes of the settlements. Some are exceptionally well preserved, as at High Rochester where not only is the base of a circular stone tomb still visible (55) but also more than eighty small barrows; excavation has shown that the latter covered burials without grave goods, apart from a few pots and coins dating from the second to early fourth centuries. Burials are recorded outside many other forts, but largely as a result of chance rather than of planned research. A great variety of burial practices is evident: cremations carried out by burning the body over the grave or off site; inhumations in lead, stone or wooden coffins, or buried without coffins in unlined pits or cists of stone or brick; graves are marked by barrows of various sizes or by stone markers or funerary monuments. Memorials to the dead ranged from rough stone slabs with crudely inscribed epitaphs through carved tombstones to large structures such as that at Shorden Brae (west of Corbridge) where a square foundation, probably the base of a tower tomb, lay within a walled enclosure surmounted by effigies of lions straddling fallen stags, eloquent of the power of death over life.

Much is thus known about types of burial practices, but because of the lack of large-scale excavations their significance is little understood. For the earlier Roman period this is as true of forts in other provinces as of those in Britain, intensive study of military cemeteries being largely restricted to fourth- and fifth-

century examples. The potential of cemetery studies is illustrated by excavations at Roman towns such as Dorchester (Poundbury), Cirencester, Colchester (Butt Road) and Winchester (Lankhills). There, in addition to recovering invaluable information about the nutrition, physique and pathology of those buried there, it has been possible to learn much about the social character of the population, for example the spread of Christianity, as at Poundbury, and the presence of Germanic mercenaries, as at Lankhills, where burials with Germanic characteristics might represent troops and their families who were part of the field army.

55 Tomb at High Rochester, consisting of a circular drum of masonry 5.2m (17ft) in diameter which was probably originally surmounted by a conical mound of earth. Much burnt material was found when the tomb was opened in the mid-nineteenth century, suggesting that it was built over a funeral pyre.

6
Supply, trade and industry

Introduction

A Roman military site with a lengthy occupation will, on average, produce far larger collections of coins, pottery, metalwork and other objects than a prehistoric or medieval site. The importance of these finds for dating the various stages in the history of a fort has long been recognized and was thus closely connected with the development of stratigraphical methods of excavation. A more recent development has been the study of finds in an attempt to reconstruct the supply systems of the Roman army. The last few decades have also seen much work on animal bones, seeds and other environmental remains. These categories of evidence shed light on two important topics. First is the question of the origin of supplies: to what extent did the Roman army depend on local agricultural production, how much of its consumable needs such as pottery was met by imports, and what effects did the demands of the army have on local economies and the economies of frontier provinces as a whole? These fields of enquiry are fundamental to understanding the position of the army in the Roman state, and particularly the demands which the army made on the resources of the Empire. The second topic concerns the living standards of the soldier: what was his diet, to what extent did he have access to imported goods and was trade between soldiers and civilians officially controlled?

Roman soldiers as consumers

That the Roman army was largely vegetarian is a hoary myth. Its origin lay in a misunderstanding of the ancient sources, which, when they refer to the military diet, harp on the lengths to which armies went to obtain adequate supplies of grain. The context is always that of an army on campaign, and grain formed the essential portable foodstuff for men and transport animals. Any archaeologist who has excavated a deeply stratified fort site will know that the circumstances of garrison life were different, for animal bones are scattered everywhere. Grain, especially wheat (56), was certainly the foundation of the military diet, but meat, although not eaten every day as analysis of human excrement from a ditch at Bearsden has shown, was frequently available.

One of the most striking aspects of the Vindolanda writing-tablets is the range of consumable items which they mention. Types of drink include vintage wine, sour wine, lees of wine, wine and honey, and Celtic beer. Food flavouring consists of lovage, garlic, spices, pepper and salt. Vegetables, pulses and fruit include beans, semolina, lentils, apples (good varieties are specified), olives, plums and radishes. All this is in addition to shellfish and varieties of meat and cereals. A much larger list could certainly be compiled from studies of the botanical and faunal remains found at other forts, but at Vindolanda the itemizing of quantities and cash values shows how these goods were obtained through a local market system. Items of clothing, even garb suitable for formal dining, could also be purchased. Many of the commodities at Vindolanda figure in documents associated with the households of the commanders. But luxury items were certainly purchased by people of lower rank. A soldier seems to have bought pepper worth two *denarii*, an import from India. As the remainder of this chapter will show, goods of the type mentioned in the Vindolanda writing-tablets reached the army on the frontiers through the operation of a complex system of supply and trade.

Granaries and supply bases

Forts of all sizes, with the exception of fortlets, contained granaries. Timber granaries are easily recognizable in excavation, for their remains usually consist of closely spaced trenches which held a grid of posts supporting a raised floor; less often, the posts are placed in individual pits, again arranged in a grid system. Stone granaries are equally unmistakeable: their walls have buttresses at frequent intervals, and the supports for the raised floors often survive in the form of parallel sleeper walls or a grid of short masonry pillars (57). At the base of the walls between the buttresses there were openings which allowed air to circulate under the raised floors. At Corbridge and Hardknott small doors gave access to the basements. They were perhaps to let dogs in to hunt for rats and mice; samples of burnt grain from the basement of a granary at South Shields contained the bones of 191 small mammals: rats, mice, dormice, voles and shrews. Granaries were intended primarily for the storage of grain, particularly wheat, but no doubt other perishable goods were stored in them as well. Their raised floors kept the

56 A wooden writing-tablet from Vindolanda containing a list of wheat and bread issued to various persons. On the reverse of this tablet is the draft petition for justice from the man from overseas who was beaten by officials; it is in the same hand as the list.

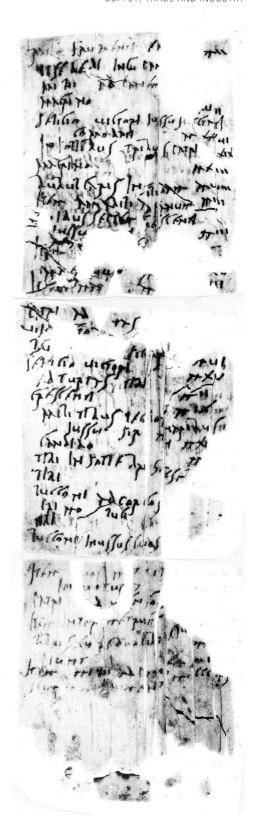

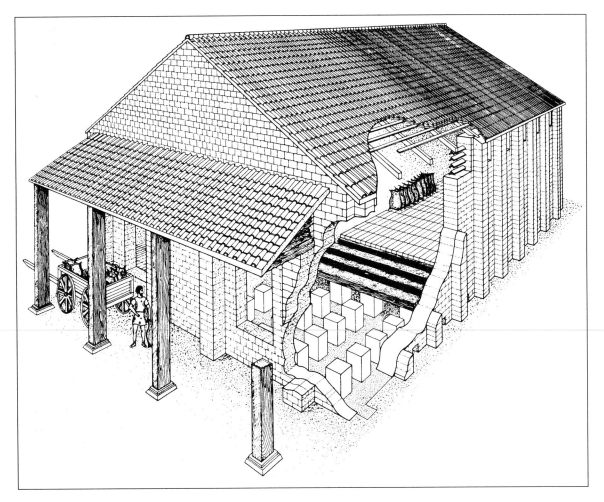

57 Reconstruction of a granary at South Shields. This granary originally served the fort built in the AD 160s and was later incorporated into the third-century supply base.

foodstuffs cool and dry, and to some extent prevented the depredations of vermin which could not be controlled by other means. The buttresses of stone granaries probably carried the main trusses of the roofs: between the buttresses there were probably wooden louvres beneath the overhanging eaves, allowing air to circulate in the interior. Access to the granaries was by means of double-leaved doors at one or possibly both of the narrow ends.

The historian Tacitus, in his biography of Agricola (governor of Britain in AD 77/8–83/4), notes that forts in newly conquered areas of Scotland held supplies to last their garrisons for a year. Numerous calculations have been made to show that fort granaries were in fact capable of holding twice the amount of grain needed in one year. In fact the capacity of granaries in forts varies and it seems that some forts held reserves far in excess of what was required for the garrison. The reason for this apparent over-provision is that the possibility of food shortages affecting the army had to be avoided at all costs. In the ancient world crop failures resulted in famine; apart from privileged groups (such as those living in the city of Rome) there was little the government could or would do to relieve suffering among the ordinary population of the provinces. A starving army, however, is an immediate and potentially overwhelming threat to the state, which was avoided by holding very large reserves of grain.

The continuing excavation of the supply base at South Shields is raising many interesting questions about the procurement system of the army. The supply base was probably built in *c.* AD 205–7, adapting a fort built in the AD 160s. At first it contained thirteen granaries, including the original double granary of the earlier fort. They were divided from the accommodation for the garrison by a wall built across the width of the fort, which was interrupted at its mid-point by the headquarters building. The supply base was built as part of the preparations for the campaigns of Emperor Septimius Severus in Scotland, providing a secure base from which grain could be shipped up the east coast to the army in the field or to intermediate supply bases such as the fort of Cramond on the Firth of Forth. In *c.* AD 222–35 the supply base was enlarged by the addition of seven more granaries, increasing its capacity from 2,081 tonnes to 3,363 tonnes of grain (58). Its main function was now to supply the garrisons of forts on Hadrian's Wall and within its hinterland, and it was probably part of a system which included supply bases at Corbridge and at a fort on the west coast, possibly Maryport. The supply base remained unaltered until the late third or early fourth century when it was partly destroyed by fire; following rebuilding, the supply base continued in use, although much reduced in size, until about the middle of the fourth century or perhaps later.

The new evidence, which shows that South Shields functioned as a supply base throughout most of the last two centuries of Roman rule in Britain, runs counter to recent thinking on the supply of grain to the army. In the 1950s and 1960s it was realized that arable cultivation during the Iron Age and Roman periods in highland areas of Britain was very extensive. That the army could thus rely on local supplies seemed a natural conclusion to draw from this new assessment of the agricultural capacity of frontier areas (59). The long duration of the supply base at South Shields means that in the case of Hadrian's Wall this view needs to be modified: although forts no doubt obtained as much grain as possible from their immediate localities, a supplementary system of long-distance supply was still necessary.

When grain is waterlogged or carbonized by fire, it survives sufficiently well to allow identification of its species. Samples from South Shields, found in deposits associated with a fire in the late third or early fourth century, have been studied by Dr M. van der Veen, who was able to show that the grain consisted mostly of spelt wheat and bread wheat. Spelt wheat had been long established as a staple crop in north-east England by the beginning of the Roman period; the samples examined also contained weed seeds typical of the region. There is as yet little evidence for the cultivation of bread wheat in north-east England and it perhaps reached South Shields from further afield. On the evidence of these samples, some of the grain stored in the supply base came from the north-east, perhaps especially from the coastal zones where settlement was dense and grain could be brought to the coast and moved to South Shields by sea; the possibility still remains that the bread wheat came from southern England or even the Continent.

Meat and fish

The abundant finds of animal bones at many forts is providing a much clearer picture of the importance of various types of animals in the military diet. The Roman period in Britain showed a general increase in numbers of cattle in comparison with the Iron Age when sheep were more important. Many of the cattle in the Roman period were of larger size and the improvements in stock were brought about at least in part by the needs of the army. Pork, fresh or cured, was also eaten in large quantities. The bones of wild animals are rare at forts, despite mention of roe deer and, less specifically, of venison in the Vindolanda writing-tablets. Fish bones are uncommon, even at coastal sites, but shellfish were consumed in large quantities. Oyster shells are often found on

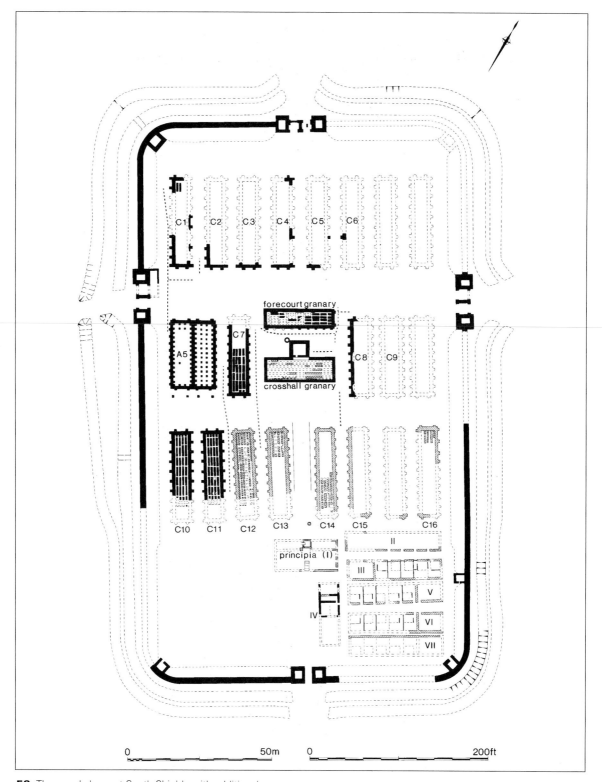

58 The supply base at South Shields with additional
granaries built in *c.* AD 222–35.

59 The Carvoran *modius* or corn measure, which carries an inscription of the emperor Domitian, dated to AD 90. Its capacity is 19.975 pints. It was used as a standard for measuring grain, most probably in the issue of military rations but perhaps also when local farmers made contributions to the army.

inland sites and a document from Vindolanda refers to oysters sent from Cordonovi, a place yet to be identified.

The study of animal bones and similar remains has long since progressed beyond mere identification of the types of animals represented. Comparative studies of the quantities of bones recovered from various types of sites, of the age at which animals were slaughtered and of the ways in which butchers prepared the carcasses can yield much valuable information about local economies. It should be possible to learn much more about the effect of military demand on animal husbandry and the economic organization of agriculture.

Industry

In frontier provinces the army was involved with industrial activities at several levels. In the years following the conquest it was directly responsible for extractive industries: for example, a lead pig from the Mendips is stamped '[product] of Nero Augustus, British [lead] – the Second Legion [produced this]'. In addition, the fort of Nanstallon, in a part of Cornwall with extensive deposits of iron, copper, silver-lead and gold, has produced crucibles, a weight and a piece of silver-rich slag. The Second Legion was perhaps also responsible for opening quarries in south-east Dorset to provide Purbeck marble for its baths in the fortress at Exeter. These quarries were worked throughout the Roman period and were exploited on an even larger scale in the medieval period. Many of these enterprises passed into the hands of civilian contractors in later years, but some at least remained under military supervision.

The army also undertook the manufacture of arms and armour. At the two legionary fortresses of Exeter and Inchtuthil, large courtyard buildings have been identified as workshops (fabricae). The plan of the fabrica at Inchtuthil has been recovered in outline by selective trenching. It measured 58.5m by 59.7m (190ft by 196ft) and consisted of aisled halls arranged around three sides of a courtyard, the fourth side being formed by a range of large rooms. Covering an area of almost 0.5ha (1 acre), this enormous building was designed for industrial activities on a formidable scale: a pit dug in one of its rooms when the fortress was abandoned before its completion contained nine iron tyres and nearly 10 tonnes of unused nails. A workshop of this size and with such a large output was to all intents and purposes a factory, a building type which does not otherwise appear in Europe until the late seventeenth and early eighteenth centuries. The fabrica at Exeter (60), although only partly excavated, provides illuminating details of manufacturing activities. It was possible to excavate only three bays of the north-eastern aisled hall and a large room at its south-eastern end. The hall contained a large number of shallow, plank-lined troughs. One contained fine sand and copper alloy powder, the by-products of turning objects on a lathe; the others contained charcoal, fragments of crucibles and copper alloy scraps. These troughs were intended to catch metal waste falling from work benches so that it could be melted down and reused. From the floor and troughs there came defective castings of copper alloy objects, including pins, a needle, a nail and a possible tie-hook used to secure strips of iron plate armour. The presence of a lathe suggests that vessels such as dishes and saucepans were also being made in this part of the fabrica. The room at the end produced no evidence of manufacturing activities; instead, around the sides of the room ran a slot, possibly for the base of cupboards or shelves where finished goods or raw materials could be stored.

Workshops have been identified in a large number of forts, but have produced little information about the activities carried out in them, usually because their interiors have not been systematically explored. In the forts at South Shields, Wallsend and Birdoswald, long narrow buildings have been found facing onto the via principalis; the comprehensive excavation of one of these buildings at

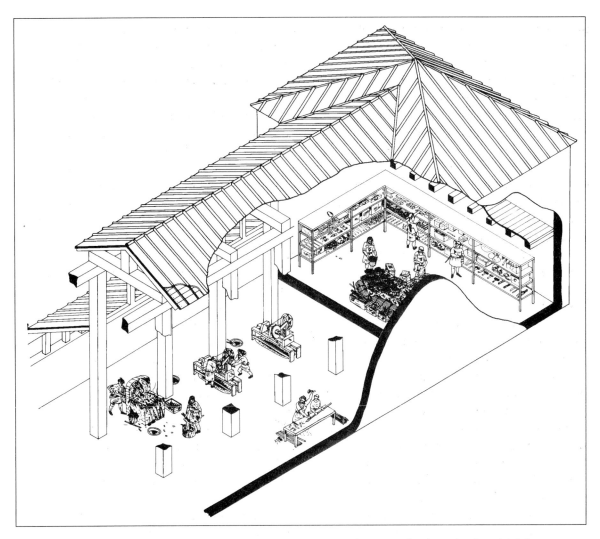

60 Conjectural reconstruction of the *fabrica* at Exeter; the aisled hall, only part of which is shown, contains lathes, a smithy and work bench, while stored in the large room at the end are raw materials and finished objects.

Birdoswald produced much evidence for metalworking. Although these buildings seem to be of a very simple type, they may have reached a considerable height, as at the legionary fortress of Regensburg in southern Germany where a long rectangular building that served as a *fabrica* stood to a height of at least 7m (23ft). *Fabricae* sometimes took the form of long buildings with short projecting wings at either end. In the west legionary compound at Corbridge there are eight such buildings .

grouped in pairs back-to-back, which have produced some debris from metalworking. Single, larger examples of this building type occur at Bearsden, Gelligaer and South Shields.

Pottery

A wide variety of pottery was used by the Roman army in Britain, ranging from fine tablewares to roughly made but serviceable kitchen wares. Pottery occurs abundantly in forts and fortresses, and in recent decades great advances have been made in its study. Its value as dating evidence has long been recognized, but a number of techniques have now been developed to extract other kinds of information from collections of pottery.

61 Left: black-burnished ware cooking pot from south-east Dorset, late third or early fourth century; south-east Dorset was an importance source of pottery for the Roman army from the second century until the second half of the fourth century. Right: a poppy-head beaker from south-east England; this drinking vessel has a polished surface and is decorated with diamond-shaped panels of applied clay dots.

Scientific analysis of the minerals included in the clays used to make pots can indicate their origin. An early application of these methods established that the two types of black-burnished wares (**61**) which supplied the bulk of the army's kitchen and ordinary tablewares throughout much of the second and third centuries AD came mainly from south-east Dorset and from Essex and north Kent (**62**).

Pottery recovered from excavations usually consists of small fragments rather than complete vessels or broken vessels which can be pieced together; these fragments can be quantified by sorting them into categories of wares which are then weighed, or by estimating the number of vessels represented by the fragments. These laborious procedures can be used to demonstrate the relative importance of various pottery manufacturing centres in supplying the army. To take as an example the two types of black-burnished ware mentioned above, work on quantification of pottery from Hadrian's Wall and the Antonine Wall showed long ago that the pottery from the kilns in Essex and north Kent was commonest at the eastern ends of the two Walls, while that from south-east Dorset was commonest at the western ends. Evidently sea-routes along the eastern and western coasts of Britain were being used to transport the pottery to the northern frontiers. That deduction was made long ago by the late John Gillam, on the basis of his careful records of the occurrences of these wares at sites on the northern frontiers. With the benefit of recent work which has quantified pottery from a wide range of sites, we now have a more complete picture of the supply of these wares. Although it is likely that most of the black-burnished ware from south-east Dorset reached the northern frontier along the western sea-routes, some at least travelled up the east coast in the earlier second century, possibly being redistributed through London. When the Antonine Wall was built, the army began to make use of the second type of black-burnished ware, drawing principally on supplies from Colchester. This ware occurs in large quantities at the eastern end of the Antonine Wall. By the third century most if not all of this ware was coming from kilns on either side of the Thames estuary, which supplied almost all the kitchen wares of forts at the east end of Hadrian's Wall. However, the ware is rare at intervening sites along the east coast, whether military or civilian, and achieved only a limited distribution in south-east England, suggesting that production was mainly aimed at the northern military market.

62 The principal sources of pottery used by the Roman army in Britain, excluding Mediterranean production sites.

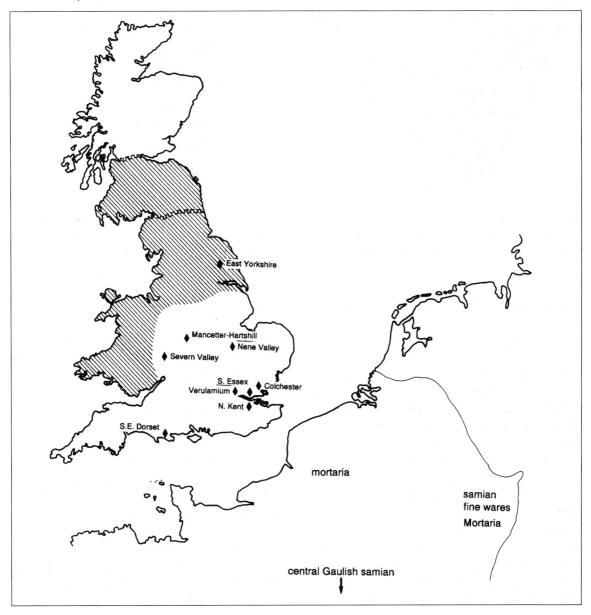

63 Fragments of mould-decorated samian ware bowls from Central Gaul, second century.

Such observations can only be made through the use of techniques of quantification, which are particularly important in analyzing the complexities of military supplies.

Another technique of study is the comparison of groups of pottery from different levels or different areas of the same site, concentrating on the function of vessels. At the Neronian fortress of Usk, vessels were classified as liquid holders, drinking vessels, table and kitchen wares, and so on. One particular area of the fortress, occupied by a courtyard building attached to an open courtyard, was shown by various statistical tests to have produced unusually large quantities of imported amphorae, used for holding liquids such as wine, olive oil and fish sauce, and equally large quantities of stoppers from amphorae. It seemed that this area was used for opening these amphorae and decanting their contents into smaller containers. When the pattern of coin finds across the excavated parts of the fortress was examined, this area also proved to have produced exceptionally large

quantities which were of unusually high denominations. This evidence seemed consistent with the use of the compound as a small market where soldiers could buy wine and other goods from traders. Apart from a reference to such trading activities in the camp of the Republican period, as described in the *Histories* of Polybius written in the second century BC, no sources mention trade within forts. Thus at Usk the pottery has illuminated, among much else, a hitherto scarcely known aspect of garrison life.

These examples show how the quantification of pottery can cast light on military supply and garrison life. However, the potential of pottery as dating evidence, which provided much of the original impetus for its study, still remains of cardinal importance. The most closely datable and intensively studied class of pottery in Roman Britain is samian ware, which was imported from various production centres in Gaul in enormous quantities from the beginning of the Roman occupation until the end of the second century AD, with some limited importation from kilns in East Gaul continuing for perhaps another fifty years (**63**). Samian ware was a fine tableware covered with a lustrous red slip; some vessels had complex decoration in relief, made by forming them in a mould, and the majority of vessels, whether plain or decorated, carried potters' stamps. The ware occurs widely in the western provinces of the Empire and its chronology is based on its occurrence in dated historical contexts, ranging from Pompeii, where an unopened crate of samian ware was retrieved from the remains of the town buried by the eruption of Vesuvius in AD 79, to Colchester where pottery shops burnt in the rebellion of Boudica in AD 60/61 have been excavated.

Samian ware is particularly useful in studying the military dispositions of the pre-Flavian and early Flavian periods. The stamps of potters working at the time can often be tied down to time spans of fifteen or even ten years, and occur in large numbers at fortresses such as Usk, Exeter and Colchester. Mould-decorated bowls can be dated with similar exactitude, and even the colour, finish and subtle variations in the shape of plain vessels can be used to distinguish Claudian from Neronian products. The presently accepted foundation dates of the early fortresses, as well as the settlement at London, depend very largely on the dating of the earliest samian.

Second-century samian ware cannot be dated as closely as earlier samian, but it still remains of value in working out the chronology of military dispositions, as is illustrated by Professor B. R. Hartley's study of the Roman occupation of Scotland published in 1972. When the Antonine Wall was constructed in *c.* AD 140, Hadrian's Wall was stripped of its troops in order to garrison the forts on the new frontier line. Until 1972 it was thought that, following a revolt by the Brigantes in *c.* AD 155, Hadrian's Wall was recommissioned, so that for a while both walls were held, the Antonine Wall being given up in the AD 180s. These conclusions were based on the sequence of occupation in forts and the interpretation of imprecise historical information. Hartley's comparison of samian ware from Hadrian's Wall and the Antonine Wall showed that much of the decorated and stamped ware from the latter was not represented on Hadrian's

Wall. There was, in fact, such a small degree of overlap that he argued that the two walls could not have been held simultaneously. He went on to propose a much simpler scheme in which the Antonine Wall was given up in *c.* AD 163, after being reoccupied for a few years following the Brigantian revolt. His conclusions have been generally accepted, although some now doubt whether there was a Brigantian revolt and a second period of occupation on the Antonine Wall.

Pottery provides valuable information about the direction and volume of trade. Because pottery was not particularly valuable, it was often used as a supplementary cargo, travelling with more bulky commodities. Samian ware is not a particularly sensitive indicator of trade, for the kilns of southern Gaul (which were succeeded in the early second century by the kilns of central Gaul), were the main suppliers of fine tablewares to the whole of Britain. Only the products of the kilns of eastern Gaul display a significant pattern of distribution, finds being concentrated in south-east England and on the northern frontier. Many East Gaulish products came from Trier and areas of the Rhineland where there were kilns making other types of pottery, such as mortaria and beakers and cups with dark metallic slips. These kilns also exported some of their output to Britain in the second and third centuries. These other wares seem to have been marketed over a wider area of Britain than East Gaulish samian: Rhineland mortaria occur throughout southern England and the dark-slipped cups and beakers are found throughout the province.

Amphorae, large double-handled containers used for transporting liquids, are another category of pottery which is important in the study of trade (64). Their contents ranged from wine to olive oil and fish sauce, all of which formed part of the military diet, and they were imported into Britain from southern Spain, southern Gaul, Italy and even from areas in the eastern Mediterranean. In the first century a wide variety of amphorae is found on military and civilian sites. In the second century the

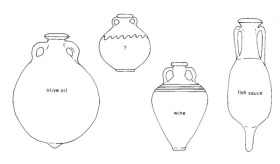

64 Types of amphora which occur on military sites: the olive oil amphora comes from southern Spain, the small amphora with a wavy line on its body from northern France (fairly rare), the wine amphora from southern France (not common on the northern frontier) and the fish sauce amphora from southern Spain and other areas.

commonest types of amphora to reach southern Britain were globular vessels from southern Spain, which contained olive oil or fish sauce, and wine amphorae from southern Gaul. It has recently been discovered that, in comparison with sites in southern Britain, the wine amphorae are rare on northern frontier sites in the second and third centuries. Wine was an essential part of the military diet and it must have been imported in containers of another type. An obvious alternative is the use of wooden barrels, remains of which sometimes survive in waterlogged levels at some forts. The Rhineland was an important wine-producing area where

barrels rather than amphorae were used to transport wine; in view of other evidence cited above for trade between this region and Britain, the Rhineland was probably the source of much of the wine used by the army on the northern frontier. This is an instance where a difference in imported goods reaching the civilian and military areas of Britain is apparent.

Although the Roman army largely depended on continental imports for its fine tablewares until the third century AD, kitchen wares were rarely imported. Wheel-thrown pottery was widespread in south-east Britain at the time of the conquest and native potters were soon supplying the army. The more crudely made wares of the Durotriges in Dorset and of the Dumnonii in west Cornwall were also used by the army; when forts were founded in north Yorkshire at the beginning of the Flavian period, the native pottery of the region (which was even cruder in technique than that of the western Dumnonii and the Durotriges) was still acceptable to the army (**65**). The large military

65 Later third-century pottery from Malton. These are probably all products of local kilns and include grey wares with polished surfaces as well as much more crudely made cooking pots differing little from those made before the arrival of the Roman army some two centuries earlier. Pottery from the local kilns was exported to Hadrian's Wall.

bases also had their own potteries; where there was no local pottery-making tradition, as at Usk, these potteries supplied the bulk of the garrison's needs. The pottery made at most of these bases shows a strong link with pottery from the Rhine frontier, where three of the four legions in Britain had been based before the conquest. Production was concentrated on kitchen wares, although some fine tablewares were made, particularly at Colchester. The potters may have been soldiers or civilian artisans who had followed the legions from Germany.

Supply from military potteries combined with the acquisition of pottery from civilian sources served the needs of the army until the early second century when there seem to have been difficulties in obtaining imported tablewares. At all three legionary fortresses the deficiency was made good by local manufacture. At Holt the legionary works depot which supplied the fortresses of the Twentieth Legion at Chester has been excavated (66); potters working there made vessels with close parallels in eastern Europe and were thus probably migrants from that part of the Empire. By the middle of the second century, however, pottery in use by the army was coming increasingly from large producers in southern Britain, particularly those making black-burnished wares. By the end of

the second century most of the pottery used by the army came from a small number of centres in southern Britain.

An interesting exception occurs at York where kilns in the immediate vicinity of the fortress were in operation in the late second to early third centuries. Some of the vessels manufactured there, and perhaps at kilns elsewhere in York, stand completely outside the Romano-British tradition of pottery. Particularly distinctive are bowls and dishes with concentric grooves or projecting flanges on their rounded bases, the purpose of which is to allow the vessels to be set securely on the projecting supports of braziers. Pottery suitable for this method of cooking is not found in the repertoires of Romano-British potters and the closest parallels for the bowls and dishes from York are to be found in the African provinces (67). African parallels are also to be found for a series of finely modelled pots in the shape of human heads, whose distribution centres on York; they date to the same period as the bowls and dishes, for the facial features and hair styles shown on several of the pots resemble portraits of Julia Domna, wife of Emperor Septimius

66 Kilns at Holt for the production of pottery, bricks, roofing tiles and other building materials.

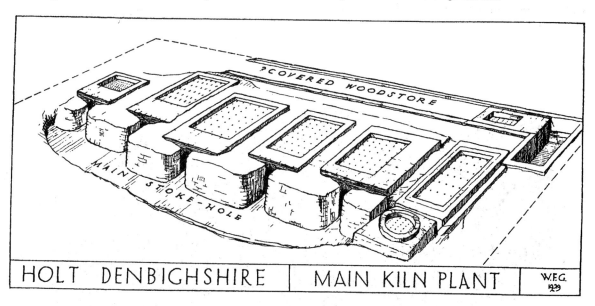

HOLT DENBIGHSHIRE | MAIN KILN PLANT | W.F.G. 1939

67 Members of the re-enactment group Quinta cooking in the style of Roman North Africa.

Severus (**colour plate 10**), and of Caracalla, the emperor's son.

In a perceptive study of these exotic pottery types Vivien Swan has shown that their appearance at York is connected with the drafting of troops from North Africa to Britain, for which inscriptions provide some evidence. The troops either included potters among their number or brought with them slave or civilian potters. Mrs Swan has also found evidence from York for the presence of potters from south-west Provence or the Languedoc, and has also found pottery of North African type at other sites, most notably the fort of Bar Hill on the Antonine Wall where such vessels were made in a kiln set in the disused stoke-hole of the baths. Another instance where pottery can be associated with the origins of troops is on Hadrian's Wall. 'Housesteads ware', found at that fort and at others in the central sector of the Wall, is identical in its forms and techniques of manufacture with native pottery from Frisia, an area in modern Holland which lay beyond the frontiers of the Empire. A unit from Frisia, the *cuneus Frisiorum*, is known at Housesteads, and dedications made by Germans or made to German gods are known from that and other sites.

7
Castra to Chester: the end of Roman forts

Introduction

One of the few Latin words current in Roman Britain which made its way into the Anglo-Saxon vocabulary was *castra*, a plural noun originally meaning a fortified camp. In the centuries following the end of Roman rule, as the distinction between military and urban fortifications was forgotten, the name came to be applied to all ancient defensive circuits. Through the conversion of *castra* into the Old English *ceaster* and then to 'chester', the Roman origins of many places are obvious from their modern names: for example, fort sites such as Chesters, Lanchester, Manchester and Chesterfield, and towns such as Dorchester, Winchester and Exeter (*Eaxanceastre*). Indeed, there are many places where the 'chester' element of their modern names remains the only indication of their origins. In this chapter the final stages of the *castra* and their transformation into 'chesters' are described.

Renewal and decline

The history of the Roman army in Britain ends in *c.* AD 410. During the previous years, the remaining effective elements of the army had been withdrawn from the island to repel barbarian attacks on Gaul and to bolster the claims of the usurper Constantine III. The Romano-British population, left defenceless, had expelled the Roman administration and organized itself against its enemies, external and perhaps also internal. In AD 410, an appeal for help went to Emperor Honorius; the reply that came back was that the cities of Britain would have to continue with their own defence unaided. This was in effect an admission that Britain was no longer part of the Roman Empire; this might have seemed to both parties a temporary state of affairs, but it was to remain permanent. That very year saw the sack of Rome by the Goths, and by AD 476 a series of military catastrophes had extinguished the Roman Empire in western Europe.

Many explanations have been advanced for the fall of the western part of the Empire. At the most obvious level, it was the result of military failures on a colossal scale: Roman provinces, one by one, were converted by force of arms into barbarian kingdoms. Of course, deeper social, political and economic reasons must be sought to explain why the Western Empire could not withstand barbarian attacks as in former times, but the part which the army played in the bloody drama of decline and fall was as important as any other factor.

The problems that faced the Roman Empire at the end of the fourth century had developed over the period of a century or more, and in the later third and fourth centuries the army underwent a series of reforms, adapting it to meet new threats. Some aspects of these reforms, particularly the reorganization of the senior command structure, are fairly well documented. Other vital aspects, such as the size and internal organization of units and their relative status and degrees of

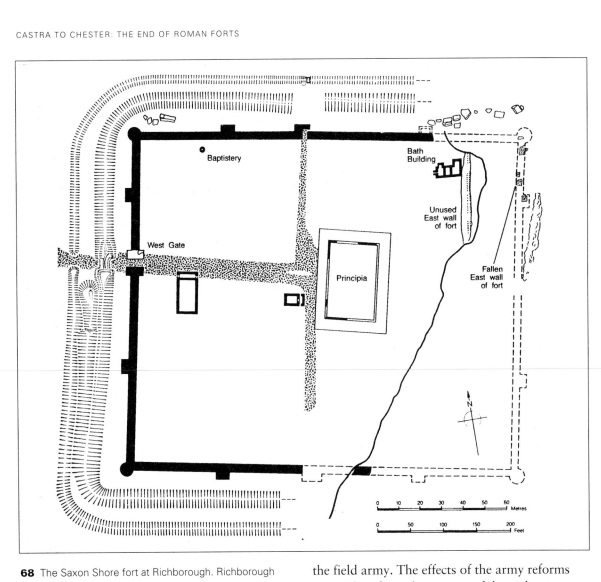

68 The Saxon Shore fort at Richborough. Richborough was the landing place of the Roman army of invasion in AD 43, later marked by the erection of a huge triumphal arch (its rectangular base can be seen in the centre of the fort); it continued as the official port of entry to Britain. Little is known of the interior plan of the Saxon Shore fort, although the base of the arch seems to have served as the foundations of the headquarters building (labelled 'principia').

competence, are poorly understood. Central to the study of the army at this period is the *Notitia Dignitatum*, a late Roman list of official posts throughout the Empire. Chapters 28 and 40 describe the military commanders in Britain, with the titles of their units and their locations; Chapter 29 lists the staff under the commander of the field army. The effects of the army reforms are evident from the content of these chapters. No longer do the legions stand at the top of the hierarchy, a position now occupied by the field army, a mobile force of elite troops. The Sixth Legion is still at York, but there is no mention of Chester and the Twentieth Legion; the Second Legion, probably reduced to 1,000 men, no longer garrisons the fortress of some 20.5ha (49.2 acres) at Caerleon, which it had occupied since AD 75, but is stationed at the Saxon Shore fort of Richborough which had an area of 2.5ha (6 acres) (**68**). The forts on Hadrian's Wall, with the exception of Burgh-by-Sands are held by cohorts and *alae*, most of which are known to have been installed in the forts by the later second or early third century. South of Hadrian's Wall, these old-style units are only found, with rare exceptions, in forts along the Cumbrian coast, which formed an extension of the Hadrian's Wall system. Most of the remaining forts in the north were occupied by units of more recent formation, designated as *numeri* and in one case as a *cuneus* (general terms for military units), or as *equites* (cavalry). Units of this type also held the Saxon Shore forts, with two exceptions: at Reculver, the garrison was *cohors I Baetasiorum*, and at Richborough the Second Legion (as already noted). These new units represent a reorganization of the army on a scale not seen since the years of conquest and consolidation. Between the AD 120s and the end of the third century, for example, we know of only three new units added to the garrison of Britain and of no more than four withdrawn for service elsewhere.

Although the *Notitia Dignitatum* serves to illustrate changes in the army, there are doubts about the exact date of the chapters that refer to Britain, and indeed it has been questioned whether all the entries are of the same date. The date of the document as a whole, on the basis of internal evidence, seems to be about AD 423. The chapters referring to Britain, no longer part of the Roman Empire after AD 410, were thus redundant in practical terms. It can be assumed that they describe the final troop dispositions in Britain, but at what date were those dispositions made? The Roman general Stilicho (by birth a Vandal) was active in Britain in AD 396–8, but it is by no means certain that he reorganized the garrisons. However, the names of some units, such as the *defensores* at Kirkby Thore, the *Solenses* at Old Carlisle and the *cataphractarii* (**colour plate 11**) at *Morbium* (possibly Piercebridge), suggest that they were detached for service in Britain from the continental field army, possibly in the AD 360s when there was much warfare in Britain.

That is as far as the document will take us, and external evidence has to be examined in order to test its validity. Inscriptions are of no help, for the latest datable example from Britain which preserves the name of a unit is an altar of

AD 270–3 from Birdoswald; by the early fourth century the practice of erecting inscribed altars, tombstones and building inscriptions had almost completely died out. Coins are useful in assessing whether the forts mentioned in the *Notitia Dignitatum* were still being held at the end of the fourth century (**69**). The latest issues to reach Britain in any quantity were coins of the House of Theodosius, dated to AD 388–402. Only sixteen forts listed in the document, just over a third of the total, have coin lists of a reasonable size (about 100 or more). Of these, four lack the latest issues: Housesteads, where there are over 500 coins from the fort, Ribchester, Lympne and Burgh Castle. Conversely, there are three forts omitted from the *Notitia Dignitatum* which have produced the latest issues: Manchester, Lancaster and Caernarvon.

The coin evidence might be dismissed on the grounds that excavators had missed the latest coins because they were in topsoil or 'squatter' occupation, usually removed without record by early excavators, or that coin supply was unreliable at the end of the fourth century (the

69 Coins of the emperors Septimius Severus and Severus Alexander (top) and Constantine (bottom). These are common issues; coins provide the best type of dating evidence from the excavation of third- and fourth-century levels in forts.

latest issues are certainly far less common on all sites except Richborough than those of the mid-fourth century). But this would be to discount the most important method of testing the usefulness of the *Notitia Dignitatum*. The question which the coins can be used to address is whether all the entries in the document are of the same date; and the answer is that on present evidence they are not. Even if the date of the British section is put back to the mid-fourth century (the date of the latest coins from Lympne and Burgh Castle), then the number of occupied forts which do not appear in the document becomes larger: Ebchester, Binchester and Ambleside have mid-fourth-century coins (as well as pottery of that date) and would therefore have to be added to the forts cited above which have the latest issues but are missing from the *Notitia Dignitatum*. A possible explanation for the occurrence of late coins in forts omitted from the document is that they had been taken over by civilians. Only large-scale excavations might establish whether this was so.

We can now turn to the archaeology of the forts to see what changes took place in the later Roman period. In the later third and fourth centuries the forts on Hadrian's Wall generally preserved their original layouts, with their defensive walls and gates, although much repaired, not substantially altered in design. The main difference was in the design of the barracks, most of which had been rebuilt by the early fourth century to conform to the later Roman type (the so-called chalets); these changes probably reflected a reduction in the size of the century which took place in the first half of the third century (see Chapter 7). Another late feature of these forts was the erection of buildings, some of them certainly barracks, on plots made available by the removal of the earth banks from behind the fort walls, as at High Rochester (see 7); these buildings might have accommodated irregular units added to the garrisons in the third century. Nevertheless, there was no overall replanning that swept away the original Hadrianic plans to

provide accommodation for new units radically different in strength and organization from the old cohorts and *alae*.

By contrast, recent excavations at South Shields have shown that in the late third or early fourth century there was a complete reorganization of at least two-thirds of the interior, providing much enlarged living accommodation (**70**). South Shields is almost certainly the *Arbeia* of the *Notitia Dignitatum*, the garrison of which was the Unit of Tigris Bargemen (*numerus barcariorum Tigrisiensium*). Its third-century garrison was the Fifth Cohort of Gauls, and the replanning of the fort was connected with the arrival of a new unit. The north-western part of the fort probably remained in use as a supply base, but the eight granaries in the central section of the fort were converted into barracks by the removal of their raised floors, the insertion of internal partitions, and the addition at their south-east ends of houses with hypocausts to accommodate the officers. South-east of the barracks was a street 7m (23ft) in width, on the other side of which were two more barracks facing onto the street. The eastern corner of the fort was occupied by a large courtyard house which was probably the residence of the commanding officer (already described in Chapter 4); one or more buildings on the corresponding plot in the southern corner were seen by the Victorian excavators, but their function is unknown. The cross-hall of the headquarters building erected in the AD 160s, which had been converted into a granary in the earlier third century, was restored to its original use, and a new rear range and forecourt were added.

The resulting plan shows the accommodation divided into four plots by two wide, intersecting streets, with the headquarters building standing at the top of the street which led to the *porta praetoria*; at least part of this street was lined with colonnades. The novelty of this plan is plain when it is compared with that which was standard for earlier forts, where the headquarters building is situated at the junction of the *via principalis* and *via praetoria*. Yet it

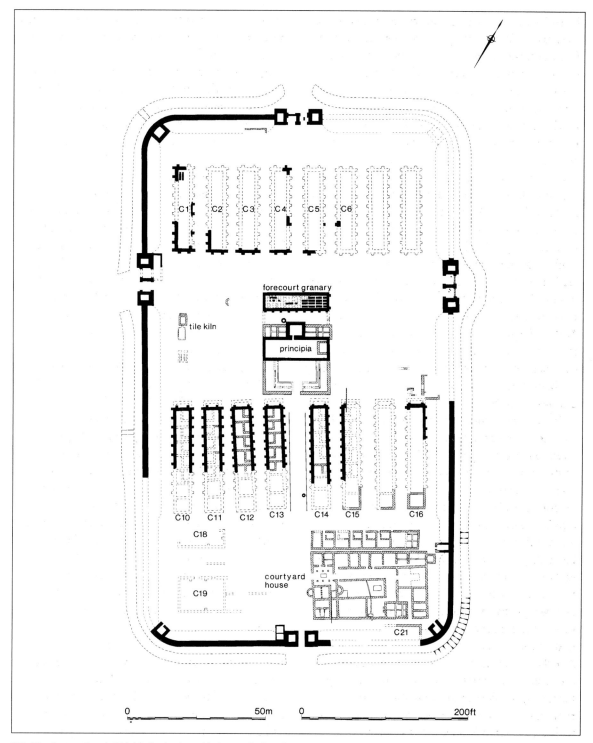

70 The fort at South Shields in the late third or early fourth century. The northern part of the fort continued in use as a supply base, while the southern part of the fort held a large garrison, accommodated in ten barrack blocks. The plan of the southern part of the fort is cruciform, with two intersecting streets dividing the interior into quarters and with the headquarters building standing at the top of the street leading from the south gate.

finds some striking contemporary parallels in very distant parts of the Roman Empire. The closest is at the Camp of Diocletian in the desert city of Palmyra in Syria, where the two intersecting streets, which are lined with colonnades, produce the same cruciform plan as at South Shields, with the headquarters building standing at the end of the *via praetoria*. The same plan also occurs at Luxor in Egypt in the ancient Pharaonic temple, whose vast halls and courts were converted into a legionary fortress in the early fourth century. This is also the plan which the soldier-emperor Diocletian used for his palace at Split (in former Yugoslavia), built for his retirement following his voluntary abdication in AD 305. All these were building projects on a monumental scale, but elements of this plan-type can be found in ordinary fourth-century forts such as Drobeta in Romania, which has a cruciform plan, or the tiny fort of Dionysias in Egypt where the headquarters building is situated at one end of the fort opposite the *porta praetoria*, from which it was reached along a colonnaded street.

The accommodation for the new garrison at South Shields thus followed a military fashion current in other parts of the Roman Empire, and thus is a counterpart to the state-of-the-art defensive architecture of the Saxon Shore forts of the same period. The plan of the fort also allows us to make a cautious estimate of the intended size of the unit for which it was built: there were ten barracks, each with five *contubernia*, which using the figure of eight men to a *contubernia* as in earlier barracks, gives a total of 400 men. By the standards of the time this was a large unit, and its status is reflected by the large, well-appointed courtyard house which seems to have been provided for its commander.

The different histories of South Shields and of the forts on Hadrian's Wall reflect the distinctions that can be made between the old- and new-style units in the *Notitia Dignitatum*. Forts south of Hadrian's Wall also show more evidence of major changes in the later Roman period than those on Hadrian's Wall, although

none has been excavated as extensively as forts such as Housesteads, Chesters and Birdoswald. Their histories have more in common with South Shields; those identifiable in the *Notitia Dignitatum* have new-style units in garrison. At Piercebridge, a new fort was built in about AD 270. It enclosed an area of 4.58ha (11 acres) and is thus far larger than other British auxiliary forts in the first and second centuries AD. The only large area to have been excavated internally is its south-east corner, which was occupied by a large courtyard house. Its position corresponds to that of the smaller courtyard house at South Shields, and this suggests that the overall plans of the two forts might have been similar. Piercebridge could have been the *Morbium* of the *Notitia Dignitatum*, which was occupied by *equites catafractarii* (heavy armoured cavalry); whatever its identification, its size shows that it was built for a very large unit, or possibly for more than one unit.

Another fort of about the same size as Piercebridge is known at Newton Kyme (**71**); it is undated and its name is not known, but it overlies an earlier fort of about 1.25ha (3 acres). North of Piercebridge on Dere Street lies Binchester, a fort of Flavian origin; whether the visible remains of its defences, which enclose an area of 3.57ha (8.6 acres) represent the outline of the original fort or a later and larger fort is uncertain. Recent excavations have shown that the large fort at Chester-le-Street (2.52ha or 6 acres) dates from the second half of the third century and replaced an earlier fort which had a turf rampart. Other forts in northern England underwent at least partial rebuilding in the later third or fourth

71 The fort and *vicus* at Newton Kyme. Inside the larger fort can be seen the south and east defences, with rounded corners, of a smaller, earlier fort. The *vicus* is associated with this earlier fort, for the south ditch of the late fort can be seen to cut through the road along which the *vicus* buildings developed. The enormous double-ditched feature east of the *vicus* is a prehistoric henge monument. It might have been converted into an amphitheatre in the Roman period.

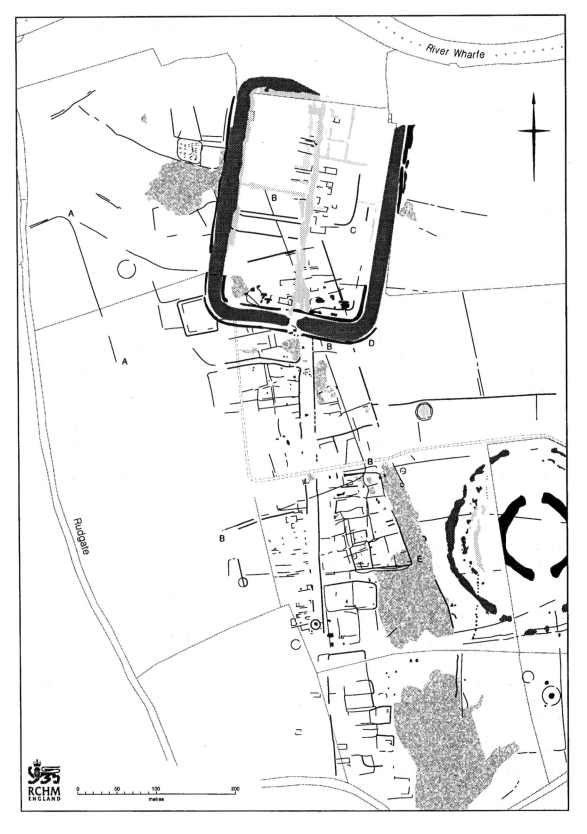

River Wharfe

A

A

B

C

B

D

Rudgate

B

B

B

E

C

RCHM
ENGLAND

0   50   100   200
metres

century, but far more excavation is required to determine how extensive the alterations were. Nevertheless, the large size of the forts at Piercebridge, Newton Kyme and Chester-le-Street shows that units of considerable strength were being added to the army in northern England during the later Roman period.

Work was also put in hand at two of the legionary fortresses. At York enormous multangular towers were added to the side fronting the river, and the headquarters was rebuilt, in part from its foundations (see **colour plate 9**). These changes, it has been suggested, might have been connected with the new office of *dux Britanniarum* (duke of the Britains), commander of all the forts in northern Britain, who perhaps set up his headquarters at York. Although there were extensive repairs to the walls at Chester, the character of the occupation in the fortress is uncertain. Occupation continued at Caerleon but on a much reduced scale.

Rebuilding of forts in the north and the construction of the Saxon Shore forts bear witness to a thorough renovation of the military defences of Britain in the closing decades of the third century, which is matched in other frontier provinces. That this period of activity virtually marked the end of military engineering on a large scale in Britain is not necessarily an argument for a speedy decline in the capacity of the army in the fourth century. It might equally be taken to demonstrate the effectiveness of the new arrangements. Decline and extinction, of course, were to be the eventual fate of the Roman army in Britain. Perhaps the first sign that resources were overstretched was the abandonment of the four outpost forts beyond Hadrian's Wall, which, on the strength of coin evidence, are thought to have been given up in the early fourth century. Their garrisons probably numbered about 2,000 soldiers, or more if irregular units of *exploratores* (scouts), known at Risingham and High Rochester (**72**), are included. There is more literary evidence for warfare in Britain in the fourth century than at any time since the initial stages of conquest and

72 The west gate at High Rochester (the blocking wall at the rear is of recent date). The fort was abandoned in the early fourth century.

pacification, and the source of those conflicts lay north of Hadrian's Wall in the lands of the Picts and Attacotti. The territory which the outpost forts had formerly controlled, providing a supervised zone beyond the Wall, might have been slipping from Roman control as the tribes to the north grew more powerful. The outpost forts would have been easily isolated by cutting the roads which linked them with the larger forces massed along Hadrian's Wall and to the south; to hold the area north of the Wall a more extensive network of forts was needed, and the necessary resources were not available.

Throughout the remainder of the first half of the fourth century there is no further evidence of withdrawals. In the following decades, however, the coin series weaken or peter out at a number of forts, as described above. Although no clear pattern is discernible, the abandonment of certain forts was probably connected with a thinning-out of the army in Britain as units were withdrawn to help deal with successive crises in other provinces in the Western Empire.

Ancient texts refer to warfare in Britain in the AD 360s, in *c.* AD 384 and in AD 396–8, but the only large-scale attempt to strengthen the defences of Britain was the construction of the Yorkshire signal-stations, probably undertaken by Magnus Maximus who seized control of the western provinces in AD 383. Four of these signal-stations are known in coastal positions, at Huntcliff, Goldsborough, Scarborough (**73**) and

Filey, and an inscription from Ravenscar, mentioning a 'tower and fort' (*turris et castrum*), signifies the presence of a fifth example. The forts were enclosures between 33m and 38m (108ft and 125ft) square with stone walls; each had a single gate and semi-circular projecting towers at each of the rounded corners of its walled enclosure. The towers at the centre of the enclosures had walls between 2m and 2.7m (6.5ft and 9ft) thick, and so probably stood several storeys high. The coastal position of these installations has always suggested that they served as lookout posts warning of sea-borne raiders: in good weather conditions major emergencies could have been signalled inland, perhaps to the garrison at Malton. They could also have been strongholds from where troops could have been sent to deal with small groups of intruders. The towers of several storeys might have accommodated thirty or forty men. Alternatively, there might have been barracks against the rear of the outer walls. At Goldsborough that is certainly suggested by a line of regularly-spaced hearths found between the tower and one of the outer walls; it is possible that the excavators missed traces of timber barracks built against the outer wall. Other towers perhaps existed further to the north, extending the system to the mouth of the Tyne, but most of the Durham coast is heavily eroded and their sites could have been long since lost to the sea.

The end of forts in Britain as part of the Roman military system is not marked by any destruction levels in their interiors. Instead, in

73 The late Roman signal station at Scarborough. The site lies within the defences of the medieval Scarborough Castle; part of the signal station has been lost to erosion of the sea cliff in the foreground.

the few forts where deposits of this period have survived, it is difficult to distinguish between the latest Roman occupation and activities in the early post-Roman period. For dating evidence after the mid-fourth century we must rely entirely on coins, and at the majority of forts these show that occupation continued into the last decade of the fourth century or the first decade of the fifth century.

Forts in fifth-century Britain

In the fifth century, Britain, after breaking its ties with Rome, entered a period still sometimes known as the Dark Ages, although many now prefer terms such as 'sub-Roman' or 'early post-Roman'. The old name may be bleakly dismissive, but it is accurate in two important respects: this period can lay claim to very few historical sources to penetrate its obscurity, and it saw the rapid extinction of Roman provincial life, in town and country alike. If any form of central control existed, military effort must have been concentrated on defending the wealthy and populous areas in southern England from Anglo-Saxon invaders, and perhaps Pictish raiders as well.

The main reasons for the abandonment of Britain were warfare and disaster in provinces nearer to Rome. It is reasonable, therefore, to assume that all effective fighting troops would have been removed from Britain. Any part of the army that was left in Britain must have been of limited military use. Deprived of pay and relying on their own efforts to feed themselves, the soldiers will have soon identified their interests entirely with their immediate locality. It is doubtful whether anything would have persuaded them to engage in the defence of other parts of Britain.

In recent years some signs of fifth-century activity have been found in forts in northern Britain. They are difficult to date precisely: there is no contemporary coinage or datable pottery and, because of a lack of suitable material, techniques such as tree-ring dating and archaeomagnetism cannot be employed.

Furthermore, at many sites ploughing or occupation in medieval and later times has destroyed the early post-Roman levels. The most informative areas have been the defensive ditches of forts and their walls and ramparts, where late deposits often survive. Thus at Housesteads, and less certainly at Birdoswald and Vindolanda, the decaying walls were encased in earth banks, and at Housesteads timber towers were set into the bank, showing that it had a military function. These banks date at the earliest to the end of the Roman period and are probably fifth-century in date (although Housesteads, where the latest coins circulating in Britain are absent, may have been fortified in this style before the end of the Roman period); they are reminiscent of the refurbishment of the ramparts of Iron Age hillforts which took place in the fifth century in parts of southern Britain, especially in the West Country. At Malton and South Shields, ditches isolated at least one of the gates of these forts in the early fifth century; at South Shields, at a still later date, a timber portal was inserted into the ruins of the gate and the ditch was filled to give access to the fort. The ditch at South Shields is larger than those of earlier periods, and resembles a large ditch of late date at Piercebridge.

These discoveries indicate that in the fifth century there were communities large enough to maintain and presumably to man defences with circuits in excess of 0.5km (a third of a mile). The nature of these communities may be demonstrated by recent excavations at Birdoswald where a large timber building was found on the site of the *via principalis* and of one of the granaries near the main west gate (74). The hall-like building resembles those found on princely sites of the fifth and sixth centuries in western Britain and suggests that Birdoswald was the seat of a local chieftain.

It would be a mistake, however, to assume that centuries of Roman military tradition were forgotten within the space of a generation or so. Procopius, a Greek historian of the mid-sixth century, describes the descendants of soldiers in

74 Conjectural reconstruction of the area inside the west gate at Birdoswald in the fifth century. The granaries have been demolished and replaced by a timber hall. The fort walls and gates survive in a dilapidated state.

Gaul in areas long under barbarian control, who even down to Procopius' own day preserved the dress and customs of their forefathers. Fifth-century occupation on Hadrian's Wall and in its vicinity might represent continuity of occupation from the late Roman period, preserving the function of the forts as local centres of power with some of the old military way of life.

Early re-use of Roman forts

Most forts in the uplands were abandoned after the end of Roman rule and were never occupied again. These were areas thinly populated before the advent of the Romans; pollen analysis shows that in the sixth and seventh centuries some of these areas were reverting to woodland. Although many fort-sites in coastal areas and the lowlands remain largely unoccupied up to the present day, some were taken over by the Church in the Anglo-Saxon period. In AD 669, Reculver was donated by a king of Kent for the foundation of a monastery, and an extensive cemetery dating from around AD 700 on the site of the fort at Newcastle upon Tyne is also probably associated with a monastery; there was probably another monastery at Chester-le-Street. At other fort-sites, later medieval churches were located in the middle of the enclosures formed by the remains of the fort defences, as for example at Bowness-on-Solway, Burgh-by-Sands and Bewcastle. Some, as at Bewcastle which has a late seventh-century cross in its churchyard, had replaced churches of Anglo-Saxon date.

However, the existence of churches as early as the seventh century on fort-sites does not necessarily suggest continuity of occupation from the Roman period. Bewcastle was abandoned a century before the end of Roman rule in Britain; Old Church, Brampton, which has a Norman church planted in the corner of the fort was given up in the early Hadrianic period. In many instances the fort defences, reduced to grassy mounds, merely formed convenient enclosures; the location of churches on the sites of headquarters buildings, which seems to hint at some form of continuity, is probably always a coincidence resulting from the central positioning of churches on fort-sites. When continuity is involved, it is more likely to be a matter of ownership rather than occupation: as at Reculver fort-sites may have been royal property, passing from the ownership of British to Anglo-Saxon kings, or were perhaps acquired because of their value as quarries for building materials.

Roman military remains in the medieval world

The ruins of Roman forts and fortresses were striking memorials of the Roman Empire, in which the origins of the medieval world were firmly rooted. When, in the late seventh century, Bede described the building of the monasteries at Jarrow and Monkwearmouth as being in the 'Roman manner' (*more Romanum*), he was certainly referring in part to the contemporary European style of construction. But his monastery at Jarrow lay two miles in either direction from the Roman forts of South Shields and Wallsend, and at the latter lay the eastern end of Hadrian's Wall, which Bede described. The monks' determination to build in stone might well have been inspired by the enduring remains of Roman military occupation in their area.

By the twelfth or thirteenth centuries most forts except in remote areas had been subjected to large-scale robbing of stone and brick for reuse in new buildings. Some structures survived because they could be adapted to serve new purposes: for example, the baths at Ravenglass were used as a house from the medieval period until fairly recent times and part of the baths of the courtyard house at Piercebridge seem to have been incorporated into a medieval chapel. At the legionary fortress of Caerleon, which must have provided far more building material for reuse than was needed, much still remained to be seen at the end of the twelfth century. In AD 1188 Giraldus Cambrensis visited the City of the Legion (which is the meaning of the name 'Caerleon') and described what he took to be the remains of immense palaces, temples and theatres. Excavations in the 1980s showed that the *frigidarium* of the fortress baths had indeed stood with its vault intact until well into the medieval period; some of the evidence for this came from deposits in the cold baths in which medieval pottery was mixed with pellets

regurgitated by owls roosting under the shelter of the vault.

Although in the later medieval period intelligible traces of Roman military occupation had generally disappeared, the Roman army was held in high regard. Vegetius' late Roman treatise, the *Military Institutions of the Romans*, was familiar to many kings and war leaders; Henry II and Richard I are said to have taken copies with them on all their campaigns, although perhaps more as an emblem of ancient military science than as a practical work of reference. The memory of Rome's imperial success was embodied in the magnificent Edwardian castle at Caernarvon which was started in AD 1283. It was built a mile distant from the Roman fort of Segontium, associated in Welsh legend with the emperors Constantine and Magnus Maximus. In the *Dream of Maxen Wledig* (a mythical figure based on Magnus Maximus) Segontium was described as a great fortified city, containing a great fort – the fairest ever seen – with great towers. The new castle at Caernarvon was meant to be the centre of English rule following Edward I's victory over the last Welsh Prince of Wales. Its architecture, with polygonal towers and courses of differently coloured stone, seems to have been inspired by the Roman walls of Constantinople, a connection reinforced by naming one of the gates the Golden Gate, the name also of one of the gates at Constantinople through which emperors entered the city on their accession or in triumph. Thus, the Roman fort and its later legendary history inspired the Edwardian architects to look back to the Roman Empire.

8
Modern study of forts

The last fifty years

The Second World War was a watershed in the development of archaeology in Britain, when bomb damage caused many opportunities for excavation in towns and cities. Little funding was available in the straitened years following the war, but important work still proved possible in London, Canterbury and elsewhere. Later redevelopments had more to do with commercial modernization than making good war damage, and more resources for archaeology were made available, especially when public taste began to turn against modern architecture of the sort favoured by developers. The most striking result of these urban excavations was the discovery of early legionary fortresses at Colchester and Exeter, buried beneath several metres of later Roman and medieval deposits. New forts were also found, perhaps most notably the Cripplegate fort in London which came to light in 1949 (75).

Equally important were the improvements in techniques to which these excavations led. Stratigraphy in towns is of a complexity rarely encountered elsewhere, and the remains of domestic buildings, especially those of the early

75 South-west corner and angle tower of the Cripplegate fort, revealed in the basement of bombed buildings in the City of London.

Roman and medieval periods, are often very slight. Systematic exploration of these deposits required a rapid development of more sophisticated methods of recording and analysis than those that prevailed in the 1920s and 1930s. In addition, the large volume of finds typical of urban excavations inspired many new avenues of research.

In the 1950s and 1960s, the Roman northern frontier was no longer at the forefront of archaeological endeavour. Hadrian's Wall was sometimes called 'a special study', and the focus of research which had developed since the late 1920s began to seem unduly narrow. Technical advances achieved elsewhere in Britain, especially in the archaeology of other periods which had once lagged far behind the excavation of Roman military sites, were not being taken up on the Roman northern frontier. Indeed, there was a degree of complacency about the study of Roman Britain in general. This is shown most clearly by Wheeler's recommendation of Roman Britain as a training ground for archaeologists: they could develop their skills on expendable sites which would add or subtract little (depending on the success of the training exercise) from the sum of knowledge; if, in Wheeler's words, they were 'Passed Roman Britain', more challenging careers were possible tackling sites in other countries which could answer fundamental questions.

In the same lecture, given in 1948, in which Wheeler belittled the study of Roman Britain, he also remarked on the large number of forts which were being discovered by aerial photography. This was to continue in the following decades. In 1936 Collingwood deplored the fact that 'only a single auxiliary fort (Margidunum) earlier than Frontinus [governor in AD 74–7] has been discovered in Britain, although scores must have existed'. He would have been disappointed to learn that the enclosure then claimed as an early fort at Margidunum is of later civilian date and that the fort, amply evidenced by military finds, is yet to be found. Some thirty years later, enough early

military sites had been found to furnish the physical evidence for the conquest of southern Britain, and archaeologists began the difficult (and, to some, questionable) task of constructing history from survey, excavation and the study of finds. Richmond, prominent in the pre-war investigations of Hadrian's Wall (see Chapter 1), had demonstrated the potential of early military sites through his excavations at Hod Hill in 1951–8; in one corner of this Dorset hillfort was a Claudian fort which Richmond demonstrated was held by a mixed garrison of legionaries and auxiliaries. Only at one other early fort in southern Britain, The Lunt at Baginton, has a comparably complete plan been recovered, but many others have been extensively sampled.

Improvements in technique, and a growing appreciation of the wealth of new knowledge which the careful application of those techniques could yield, soon made an impression on the Roman northern frontier. Daniels' publication of the Red House baths at Corbridge (see **50**) embodied a fully modern approach, and Gillam revived the study of coarse pottery, vital to the dating of sites and to analyses of trade and economy. But the 1960s saw the beginnings of new developments in archaeology that were rooted in other periods. These had much to do with quantification and the statistical manipulation of data, and have grown in importance as information technology has become more readily available. At the same time archaeologists have appropriated and adapted systems of thought from the social sciences in order to try to make better sense of their information. There are many areas of archaeology later than the prehistoric period where the impact of these new ideas has been patchy, among which Roman military archaeology is certainly to be numbered. Parallel changes have occurred in the study of ancient history, and they often indicate more profitable lines of research for Roman military archaeologists than those connected with insular British archaeology. Analyses of Roman frontier systems, of the relationships between native communities at the edges of the Empire and

Roman culture (largely in the form of the army), and of the organization and economic effects of army supply are all areas of study by ancient historians who rely largely on archaeology to supply further evidence for consideration.

The 1970s saw the climax of archaeological activity in Britain. Government funding for rescue archaeology had grown enormously and an increasing number of developers were contributing voluntarily to the costs of excavations on threatened sites; universities, museums, state agencies and archaeological trusts all played a part in this upsurge of archaeological endeavour. Economic recessions and a greater willingness to limit or prevent the destruction of archaeological sites in the course of building developments have changed everything. Opportunities for development in the historic cores of towns and cities are now very few, for most areas that have not been comprehensively redeveloped are protected by conservation orders. There are few opportunities for excavations which will make solid contributions to knowledge; the full value of information which emerges from small-scale archaeological assessments is usually only to be realized when fuller excavations follow. Many Roman forts lie beneath towns and it is unlikely that we shall learn much about them in the foreseeable future.

Forts in open landscapes usually have protected status as Scheduled Ancient Monuments. There are a number of programmes of research on such forts, as in recent years at Newstead, Birdoswald, Vindolanda and South Shields, but funding for such projects is very difficult to obtain. The contributions which such excavations can make to our knowledge of the Roman army, and indeed of Roman society in general, is nowhere more strikingly evident than at Vindolanda.

Vindolanda

Throughout the previous chapters several references have been made to the Vindolanda writing-tablets. They deserve special mention in any account of Roman forts in Britain. Chesterholm, now usually known by its Roman name of Vindolanda, was a fort built in the middle to late AD 80s on the Stanegate, a road which by the early second century AD formed the main east–west route in the northern frontier zone. The fort continued in use when Hadrian's Wall was built a short distance to the north of the Stanegate and was occupied down to the end of the Roman period. Excavation had taken place in the 1930s, mostly within the later stone fort. In 1967 Robin Birley began his excavations which were to lead to the recovery of by far the most extensive plan of a *vicus* known in Britain. In 1972, in digging a drain to deal with ground water, a thick layer of clay was found beneath the *vicus* buildings; when penetrated, the clay was seen to overlie deep organic deposits. Work in succeeding years showed that these deposits belonged to a series of early timber forts, and that wood, leather, textiles and many other kinds of organic material survived intact. The processes which contributed to this exceptional degree of preservation are not fully understood, but an anaerobic environment (i.e. excluding air) coupled with the presence of large amounts of tannin and other substances seem to have been important factors.

Sites of this type are always of great interest, for they provide a wealth of environmental evidence as well as artefacts which never survive in normal conditions. What makes Vindolanda exceptional, however, is the recovery of a large number of wooden writing-tablets. Before the Vindolanda discoveries, the only documents known to have survived from Roman Britain were a few wooden stylus tablets; these have a rectangular recess filled with black wax on which the text was incised, its preservation depending on whether the point of the stylus penetrated through the wax into the wood. Writing-tablets are wafer-thin sheets of wood with carefully smoothed surfaces.

The Vindolanda writing-tablets, 194 of which have been published, give an astonishingly varied picture of life in a frontier fort in the late first and early second centuries AD. The texts were written by prefects, other officers, ordinary soldiers, slaves and traders, and also include the earliest known examples of handwriting in Latin by a woman. Their subject matter is equally varied: some are routine reports or requests for leave couched in formulaic language, in effect standard administrative forms; the remainder, of more interest, are letters on social, military, business and quasi-legal subjects, inventories or military rosters. They supply us with the names of the garrisons at Vindolanda and in one case their actual strength; daily reports tell us what tasks occupied the soldiers. These and similar aspects of the writing tablets have been referred to in previous chapters, but their contents are also important for other fields of study. The development of handwriting and the evolution of the Latin language are also illuminated by the Vindolanda tablets.

Recent years have also seen the recovery of documents from other sites, notably a large series of lead curse tablets from the Sacred Spring at Bath, which provides a civilian complement to the Vindolanda tablets. The early fort at Carlisle has also produced some documents, among them a loan agreement made by two soldiers of the Twentieth Legion.

These discoveries make it certain that in years to come the study of Roman Britain, and especially the activities of the army, will be supported by an archive of everyday documents, a circumstance which would have seemed incredible thirty years ago. Such an archive has the potential to provide detailed information about questions for which other areas of study can supply only vague or general answers, for example unit sizes as deduced from the planning of forts. This is not to say that the retrieval of tablets will ever supersede excavations recorded and interpreted to the most rigorous standards. One of the most important aspects of the Vindolanda tablets is their context. The only comparable collections of documents are from Egypt and Syria and in many cases little is known about their discovery; indeed, one of the most interesting collections, the archive

of Flavius Abinnaeus who was a mid-fourth-century fort commander, was purchased in Egypt from dealers in antiquities. The find spots of the Vindolanda tablets are precisely recorded in and around buildings of several successive periods, and were found in association with many other objects. The archaeological context of the tablets add much to the significance of their contents. For example, four tablets found in what is suggested to be the centurion's quarters in a barrack of Period 4 (c. AD 104–20) might well represent documents of a trader involved in army supply. This seems to have been a risky business, for one of the documents is an anguished appeal to a high official, probably the governor, by 'a man from overseas and an innocent one' who had been beaten with rods, probably by a centurion, and had sought redress in vain from other local officers. On the other side of the tablet, written in the same hand, is a list of quantities of wheat issued to various people; two of the other tablets are records of dealings in other goods, and the third tablet is a long letter concerning, among other matters, the purchase of a very large quantity of grain.

Why these documents ended up in a supposed centurion's quarters is one of very many questions about the contexts of the Vindolanda documents. Why are private and official documents promiscuously mingled? Why do letters written by slaves, traders, ordinary soldiers and commanders appear in the same part of the fort? The key to these and many other questions depends on further research.

Presenting Roman forts to visitors

The Romans are seen by the public as great builders and engineers, whose over-indulgence in a cruel and luxurious society led to their decline and fall. The Romans built roads, had centrally heated houses, threw Christians to the lions, built Hadrian's Wall and maintained a formidable standing army. Except for the notion that the Romans were exceptionally depraved, none of these perceptions is wrong, but it is the task of the museum curator and of other interpreters of the

heritage to explain the rich complexity of the Roman world that lies behind the popular images.

Roman forts in spectacular settings, such as Hardknott (76) and Housesteads, have always been popular with visitors. In recent decades other less well-known forts have attracted increasing numbers of visitors. This is partly a result of improved presentation at those sites and partly to do with the needs of schools studying the Romans as part of the National Curriculum. Until the 1970s the presentation of archaeological sites was usually very austere. Apart from plaques giving the names of the buildings, there were no information boards apart from a notice reminding visitors of the severe penalties awaiting those who defaced or damaged the remains. The guide books usually available were of impeccable scholarship but assumed prior knowledge of the subject.

A new approach, based on site reconstructions, developed in the later 1960s. At The Lunt, Baginton, a length of turf rampart was reconstructed in 1966, to be followed in 1970 by a timber gate and in 1973 by a granary.

76 The Roman fort at Hardknott perched dramatically on the edge of a precipitous slope above Eskdale. The modern road follows the Roman route across the mountain passes from the fort of Ravenglass on the coast to the fort at Ambleside on Lake Windermere. Forts in such magnificent natural settings have always been a magnet for visitors.

Reconstructions were also built at Vindolanda, where the Vindolanda Trust also set up direct links with local education authorities. Helped by outstanding archaeological discoveries, Vindolanda soon became one of the most popular sites in the Hadrian's Wall area.

A separate development has been the trend to make museum displays more attractive to visitors. Audio-visual presentations, computer interactives and new ways of displaying and interpreting objects can create exhibitions of great appeal. There certainly remains a place for traditional museums where the objects can be contemplated without a barrage of intrusive information; the site museum at Chesters, organized somewhat eccentrically by a famous

77 Interior of the museum at Chesters, little altered since the objects were first displayed in c. 1900.

Egyptologist at the beginning of this century, is impressive by virtue of the sheer quantity of material on display (**77**). A common theme of modern museum displays is interaction and role-playing: visitors are encouraged to empathize with the people who made and used the objects which are displayed. This is a way of attempting to reconstruct the past which is mirrored by the

78 Cardiff Castle. The walls of this late Roman fort were completely rebuilt a century ago to provide a setting for the extravagant Victorian castle of the Marquesses of Bute.

physical reconstruction of forts. The walls and one gate of the late Roman fort at Cardiff were reconstructed a century ago (**78**); the first thoroughly researched reconstructions at The Lunt, Baginton, and at Vindolanda, were followed by others at Manchester and South Shields (see **colour plate 5**). Another aspect of reconstruction is provided by re-enactment societies which seek to replicate the arms and equipment and military tactics of the legions and auxiliary cohorts (see **colour plate 11**).

Reconstruction is worthless unless it is based on thorough research. If properly done, it can stimulate the imagination of visitors far more successfully than conventional museum displays and publications. Many forts are poorly preserved and the reconstruction of even a small part of such a site can give scale and meaning to the other remains. The surroundings and later histories of forts must be taken into account; reconstructions could not be added to the inspiring landscape of Housesteads but might be acceptable in an urban or suburban setting. Some archaeologists, it has to be admitted, are still hostile to this approach to the presentation of a site, even when it is carried out in strictly controlled circumstances. The fear still lingers that reconstructions will destroy, conceal or distort archaeological evidence.

The future

The discoveries at Vindolanda show how much information about the Roman army still remains to be recovered by excavation. The spectacular nature of these discoveries, however, must not be allowed to overshadow advances in archaeological techniques, the potential of which is only beginning to be realized. Perhaps the most important is geophysical prospection, which, although by no means a recent innovation, has benefited from the introduction of more sensitive equipment enhanced by the application of information technology. More than three-quarters of the plan of the fort at Lanchester has been traced in telling detail with the use of a fluxgate gradiometer. Similar

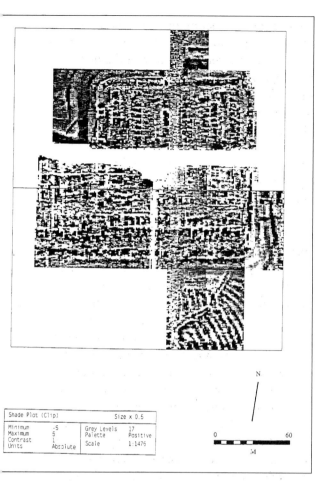

Shade Plot (Clip)   Size x 0.5

Minimum	-5	Grey Levels	17
Maximum	5	Palette	Positive
Contrast	1	Scale	1:1476
Units	Absolute		

0   60

M

79 Plot of magnetometer survey of the fort of Halton Chesters on Hadrian's Wall. Walls show as lighter areas; ditches and the interiors of buildings are darker. The interpretation of these results requires much careful work, but some parts of the fort appear very clearly, particularly the north-west part of the fort defences.

surveys at other forts, as at Halton Chesters (**79** and **80**), have produced plans which are more fragmentary but still of great value. Ground radar has recently been used successfully in archaeology; it produces a series of vertical sections, penetrating to the base of the very deepest stratigraphy, and therefore complements established techniques of geophysical prospection which are of limited use on sites with complex stratigraphy. When compared with the costs of excavation, these techniques are very inexpensive. Their disadvantage is that

they produce plans which have much the same value as those recovered by Victorian excavators (although that value is by no means negligible): there is a skeleton of walls and other features, but the flesh of stratigraphy is missing, and it is that which provides dating evidence, allows different structural periods to be distinguished and identifies the uses of buildings.

Much information recovered by excavation has yet to be analyzed. In recent years English Heritage has supported the publication of reports on state-funded excavations from past decades, as well as important excavations funded from other sources. At the same time the surface remains of military sites have been comprehensively surveyed, many for the first time. When full publication of old excavations is combined with geophysical survey, a systematic study of archives and a complete catalogue of finds (as is the case with an increasing number of fort sites), then further knowledge can be gained only by excavation. This ultimate and most exciting venture into archaeological scholarship is a fateful one, for it involves the physical destruction of a site, leaving at best only a skeleton of walls. Moreover, it is expensive, time-consuming and requires practical and theoretical skills which can only be acquired in the field.

Research excavations have to be justified in detail, balancing the need to preserve sites against present demands for new knowledge. There is a presumption in favour of preservation which can only be displaced by an overwhelmingly strong case for excavation which meets widely accepted research objectives and is sufficiently well funded to achieve the highest possible standards. There can be no argument about the need to continue recording sites in advance of their destruction by building development, but there are many questions which such excavations will never answer. Research frameworks are at present very much in fashion and there are certainly important areas of forts, such as the cemeteries and *vici*, which have not received sufficient attention in the past. To recommend that most of our resources in the near future should be concentrated on such areas, however, would be mistaken. In the case of cemeteries the expectation is that burial rites and techniques such as DNA testing will allow ethnic and family groups to be identified, and that much will be learnt about diseases, nutrition and longevity. The importance of such work would plainly be greatly diminished if little was known about the associated forts and their garrisons. Likewise, the significance of fluctuations in the population of a *vicus* would be difficult to assess without detailed knowledge of its fort. The greatest advances in knowledge will in fact be achieved by comprehensive excavations of forts and their settings, so that each element – fort, *vicus*, cemetery and hinterland – will illuminate all the others.

The resources for such projects will always be scarce but there is much that can usefully be done on a smaller scale by professional and amateur archaeologists alike. There are still forts to be discovered: in 1996 two were found in Cumbria and Norfolk. Few will be fortunate enough to find new forts but progress is always made by the accumulation of small details. Field-walking and survey, the study of the environs of forts and of Roman roads, and the analysis of objects such as pottery and metalwork, will all contribute to the growth of the subject.

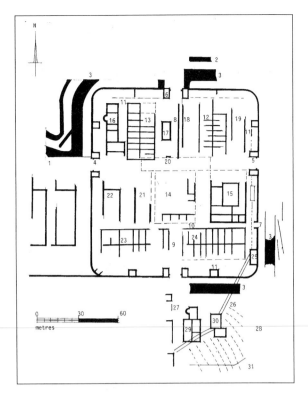

80 Interpretation of the Halton Chesters magnetometer survey (see **79**). A modern road crosses the fort, obscuring Hadrian's Wall which joined the sides of the fort at right angles immediately south of the gates. The continuation of the south wall of the fort to the west is obvious; excavation has shown that at some stage the west wall south of the gate was demolished to form an enlargement of the fort, its north side formed by Hadrian's Wall.

Dating by emperors and imperial houses, AD 41–235

Dates in the Roman period are often cited by reference to the reigning emperor or to imperial houses, especially in the earlier Roman period.

AD	EMPEROR	PERIOD
41–54	Claudius	Pre-Flavian
54–68	Nero	
68–9	Galba, Otho, Vitellius	
69–79	Vespasian	Flavian
79–81	Titus	
81–96	Domitian	
96–8	Nerva	
98–117	Trajan	
117–38	Hadrian	
138–61	Antoninus Pius	Antonine
161–80	Marcus Aurelius	
177–92	Commodus	
193–211	Septimius Severus	Severan
198–217	Caracalla	
218–22	Elagabalus	
222–35	Severus Alexander	

Sites and museums to visit

Few early fort sites in England and Wales survive as visible earthworks, but some museums display objects from early forts, often with plans and models. Remains of some stone-built forts are far better preserved but there are still many sites where little or nothing is visible. The list of sites and museums below is highly selective; R. J. A. Wilson's *A Guide to the Roman Remains in Britain* (3rd edn, 1988) describes all the sites with significant visible remains.

South-east England

Portchester, Pevensey, Lympne and Richborough: the best preserved forts in the Saxon Shore system.
London: the Museum of London has tombstones and other objects associated with soldiers, some of whom were stationed at the Cripplegate fort which is near the Museum at London Wall (fragments of fort wall are visible). The British Museum displays some of the Vindolanda writing-tablets and other finds from military sites.

South-west England

Hod Hill: a remarkable example of an early Roman fort set in one corner of a native hill-fort.
Old Burrow and Martinhoe: early fortlets on the North Devon coast.
Exeter, Taunton, Dorchester, Cirencester and Gloucester: museums with objects from early military sites.

Wales

Cardiff: the National Museum of Wales has objects from many military sites; nearby is a late Roman fort (Cardiff Castle), its walls largely reconstructed in the late nineteenth century.
Caerleon: parts of the baths, barracks and defences of the legionary fortress are visible; the amphitheatre outside the fortress has been completely uncovered. There is an excellent site museum.
Brecon Gaer: gates and fort wall visible.
Tomen-y-Mur: earthwork remains of fort, amphitheatre and parade ground.
Caernarfon: extensive remains of fort, site museum and separate supply base (Hen Waliau).
Caer Gybi: walls of a small late Roman fort.

Central England and East Anglia

Chester: the walls of the fortress, exceptionally well preserved, scanty remains of internal buildings, and external amphitheatre, the largest in Britain. The Grosvenor Museum has a fine collection of objects from the fortress.
Wroxeter and Lincoln: museums, but visible remains belong to the Roman towns.
The Lunt, Baginton: timber fort with reconstructed gate, rampart, granary and circular enclosure (probably for schooling horses and riders), display of objects.
Burgh Castle: impressive remains of Saxon Shore fort.

Northern England, south of Hadrian's Wall

York: part of the headquarters building is visible in the undercroft of the Minster; objects from the fortress are displayed in the Yorkshire Museum, near multangular tower at the western corner of the fortress.

The most instructive fort sites are: *Ribchester* (mainly the museum), *Lancaster*, *Ambleside*, *Hardknott* (stirring mountain setting), *Ravenglass* (baths), *Maryport* (museum), *Manchester* (reconstructed gate), *Cawthorn* (fort and temporary camps), *Scarborough* (Yorkshire Coast signal station), *Piercebridge*, *Binchester*, *Old Carlisle*.

Hadrian's Wall zone

At the following forts extensive remains are visible and each has a site museum: *South Shields, Wallsend, Corbridge, Chesters, Housesteads, Vindolanda, Birdoswald*. See also *Benwell* and *Carrawburgh* for temples. The best-preserved stretches of Hadrian's Wall lie between Chesters and Birdoswald, although some turrets are visible west of Birdoswald and fragments of the Wall can be seen in the first 20 kilometres (12 miles) of its course through urban Tyneside.

Newcastle upon Tyne and Carlisle: important museum collections.

Scotland and England north of Hadrian's Wall

South of the Antonine Wall forts at *High Rochester, Chew Green* (small fort and temporary camps) and *Birrens* (with the nearby siegeworks at *Burnswark*) are worth visiting.

Much of the Antonine Wall lies in urban areas: the most interesting remains are at *Rough Castle* but there are remains worth seeing at *Bar Hill* and *Bearsden*.

North of the Antonine Wall the earthwork remains of *Ardoch* are spectacular; *Inchtuthil* has slight remains, but sufficient to convey the great size of a legionary fortress.

Further reading

The fullest account of Roman Britain is still S. Frere's *Britannia* (rev. edn, RKP 1987); for a shorter account, see M. Todd, *Roman Britain* (Fontana 1981). M. Millett's *The Romanization of Britain* (Cambridge University Press 1990) is a penetrating analysis of the processes of Romanization, overly sceptical about the army's role outside southern England; see also his *Roman Britain* (Batsford/English Heritage 1995). S. Esmonde Cleary's *The Ending of Roman Britain* (Batsford 1989) describes the final century of Roman rule.

General works on the Roman army are G. Webster, *The Roman Imperial Army* (Batsford 1985), Y. Le Bohec, *The Imperial Roman Army* (Batsford 1994) and G. Watson, *The Roman Soldier* (Thames and Hudson 1969). Central to the study of Roman forts in Britain is A. Johnson's *Roman Forts* (A and C Black 1983), dealing only with the first and second centuries; shorter but more wide-ranging treatments are R. Wilson's *Roman Forts* (Bergstrom and Boyle 1980) and D. Breeze's *Roman Forts in Britain* (Shire Books 1983). The recently published *Roman Camps in England* by H. Welfare and V. Swan (HMSO 1995) includes incidentally plans and descriptions of forts; S. Frere and J. St Joseph's *Roman Britain from the Air* (Cambridge University Press 1983) has aerial photographs and descriptions of forts.

Works which include descriptions of specific groups of forts include D. Breeze and B. Dobson, *Hadrian's Wall* (3rd edn, Penguin 1987), S. Johnson, *Hadrian's Wall* (Batsford/English Heritage 1989), M. Jarrett (ed.), *The Roman Frontier in Wales* (2nd edn, University of Wales Press 1969), C. Daniels (ed.), *Handbook to the Roman Wall* (13th edn, H. Hill 1978), W. Hanson and G. Maxwell, *Rome's North West Frontier: The Antonine Wall* (Edinburgh University Press 1986), S. Johnson, *The Roman Forts of the Saxon Shore* (Elek 1976), V. Maxfield (ed.), *The Saxon Shore: A Handbook* (University of Exeter Press 1989).

For specific aspects of fort architecture, see A. Gentry, *Roman Military Stone-Built Granaries in Britain* (Brit Archaeol Rep 32, 1976), M. Jones, *Roman Fort Defences to AD 117* (rev, edn, Brit Archaeol Rep 21, 1977), P. Bidwell, R. Miket and B. Ford, *Portae Cum Turribus: Studies of Roman Fort Gates* (Brit Archaeol Rep 206, 1988) and D. P. Davison, *The Barracks of the Roman Army from the 1st to 3rd Centuries AD* (Brit Archaeol Rep Int Ser 472, 1989).

There are many hundreds of articles and books describing individual forts. The following are publications from the last decade or so which include general accounts of forts or illuminate specific aspects of fort development:

P. Austen, *Bewcastle and Old Penrith: A Roman Outpost Fort and Frontier Vicus* (CW Res Ser 6, 1991).

P. Bidwell and S. Speak, *Excavations at South Shields Roman Fort, Vol 1* (Soc Antiq Newcastle-upon-Tyne Mon Ser 4, 1994).

R. Birley, *Vindolanda Research Reports, New Series, I–III* (Vindolanda Trust, 1993–4) for the pre-Hadrianic forts. See also A. K. Bowman, *Life and Letters on the Roman Frontier: Vindolanda and its People* (British Museum Press 1994) and A. K. Bowman and J. D. Thomas, *The Vindolanda Writing-Tablets (Tabulae Vindolandenses II)* (British Museum Press 1994). For the later stone forts, see P. Bidwell, *The Roman Fort of Vindolanda* (HBMC(E) Archaeol Rep 1, 1985).

M. Bishop and J. Dore, *Corbridge: Excavations of the Roman Fort and Town* (EH Archaeol Rep 8, 1988): full account of the first- and second-century forts.

P. Casey and J. Davies with J. Evans, *Excavations at Segontium (Caernarfon) Roman Fort, 1975–1979* (CBA Res Rep 90, 1993).

J. Crow, *Housesteads* (Batsford/English Heritage 1995).

S. S. Frere and J. J. Wilkes, *Strageath: Excavations within the Roman Fort, 1973–86* (Britannia Monongraph 9, 1989).

P. Ottaway, *Roman York* (Batsford/English Heritage 1993). See also D. Phillips and B. Heywood, *Excavations at York Minster, Vol 1* (HMSO 1995): excavation of the headquarters building and barracks.

L. Pitts and J. St Joseph, *Inchtuthil: The Legionary Fortress* (Alan Sutton 1985).

Index

Bold page numbers refer to illustrations. Numbers in brackets following fort names refer to the key to the location maps given on page 13.

The Author

Paul Bidwell is Head of Archaeology for Tyne and Wear Museums. He has excavated widely on Roman military sites in south-west England and on Hadrian's Wall and in its vicinity. His publications include major reports on sites at Exeter, Vindolanda, Chesters and South Shields.

At present he is responsible for extensive excavations at South Shields and Wallsend and is working with architects to finalize plans for the reconstruction of a military bath-house at the latter site.

> 'One of the great classic series of British archaeology.' *Current Archaeology*

This volume is part of a major series, jointly conceived for English Heritage and Batsford, under the general editorship of Dr Stephen Johnson at English Heritage.

Titles in the series:

Sites
Avebury Caroline Malone
Danebury Barry Cunliffe
Dover Castle Jonathan Coad
Flag Fen: Prehistoric Fenland Centre Francis Pryor
Fountains Abbey Glyn Coppack
Glastonbury Philip Rahtz
Hadrian's Wall Stephen Johnson
Housesteads James Crow
Ironbridge Gorge Catherine Clark
Lindisfarne Deirdre O'Sullivan and Robert Young
Maiden Castle Niall M. Sharples
Roman Bath Barry Cunliffe
Roman London Gustav Milne
Roman York Patrick Ottaway
St Augustine's Abbey, Canterbury Richard Gem et al.
Stonehenge Julian Richards
Tintagel Charles Thomas
The Tower of London Geoffrey Parnell
Viking Age York Richard Hall
Wharram Percy: Deserted Medieval Village Maurice Beresford and John Hurst

Periods
Anglo-Saxon England Martin Welch
Bronze Age Britain Michael Parker Pearson
Industrial England Michael Stratton and Barrie Trinder
Iron Age Britain Barry Cunliffe
Norman England Trevor Rowley
Roman Britain Martin Millett
Stone Age Britain Nicholas Barton
Viking Age England Julian D. Richards

Subjects
Abbeys and Priories Glyn Coppack
Canals Nigel Crowe
Castles Tom McNeill
Channel Defences Andrew Saunders
Church Archaeology Warwick Rodwell
Life in Roman Britain Joan Alcock
Prehistoric Settlements Robert Bewley
Roman Forts in Britain Paul Bidwell
Roman Towns in Britain Guy de la Bédoyère
Roman Villas and the Countryside Guy de la Bédoyère
Ships and Shipwrecks Peter Marsden
Shrines and Sacrifice Ann Woodward
Victorian Churches James Stevens Curl

Towns
Canterbury Marjorie Lyle
Chester Peter Carrington
Durham Martin Roberts
Norwich Brian Ayers
Winchester Tom Beaumont James
York Richard Hall

Landscapes through Time
Dartmoor Sandy Gerrard
Peak District John Barnatt and Ken Smith
Yorkshire Dales Robert White
Forthcoming
Lake District Robert Bewley